LIFE IN JAPAN

LIVING AND WORKING IN JAPAN

Brief history and behavior of Japanese people

Kiri Amarakoon

ISBN: 9798392787005
Imprint: Independently published

DEDICATION

I dedicate this book to my parents, my family, and the Xerox Corporation for the opportunity given to me and my family to experience life in the unique country of Japan.

Table of Contents

Preface

It has been 40 years since we lived in Japan. I have been planning on writing this book for some time and after I published my book about the overland car trip from England to Sri Lanka in 1970 on Amazon Kindle Publishing I was encouraged to write our family experiences and about our life and working with a team of Japanese Engineers. Our children were five and eight years old their experience and my wife's experiences are also included .

The book also contains a brief geography and history of this unique country and its inhabitants dating back to the prehistoric period. Included in the book also are the uniqueness of Japan of their language and behavior compared to the three other countries I had the pleasure of living and working in.

Most of the Japanese and other non-English words are in Italics throughout the book usually when seen for the first time. These are listed in the index with meaning and pronunciation where possible.

The abbreviation AD stands for the Latin phrase Anno Domini, which means "in the year of our Lord." You'll often see AD placed before or after a number to refer to a year after the birth of Jesus Christ. CE stands for "Common Era." It refers to the same years as AD does, just in a more secular way. The year 2022 CE is the same year as 2022 AD.

ACKNOWLEDGMENTS

While writing this book, I needed help from various sources. I wish to thank them for their contributions.

My wife and children provided me with their experiences and feeling regarding the life and surroundings of the country, mostly around Tokyo.

My good friend and colleague Akira Miyazaki I had the pleasure of meeting at the Fuji Xerox office helped me to confirm and correct some of my descriptions and geographical details. We continue to communicate with each other.

Introduction

The main purpose of this section is to convey the historical background as it relates to the wonderful opportunity to live and work in Japan with my family.

I grew up in a small remote village in the hilly countryside, known as the "upcountry" eight miles from the nearest large town Kandy, the ancient capital of Sri Lanka before invasions by the European Empire builders such as the Portuguese in 1505, the Dutch in 1656 and finally the British in 1815. They eventually took control of Kandy town and made Colombo the Capital city. In 1802 Ceylon became a crown colony and was ruled for further 133 years until gaining independence in 1948 without violence.

The Portuguese

Portuguese invaded the country in 1505 and found no serious opposition. Founded the port of Colombo in 1517 and extended control over the coastal areas. The indigenous Sinhalese set up Kandy as the capital and was never conquered by the invaders. Portuguese missionaries converted lowland Sinhalese to Christianity. The Buddhist majority disliked the Portuguese and the king sought help from the Dutch who landed in 1602.

The Dutch

Dutch signed a treaty with king Ranasinghe II in 1638 to get rid of the Portuguese on the condition that they had a monopoly of trade over the island. They captured Colombo from the Portuguese in 1656. By 1660 they controlled the whole island except the land-locked kingdom of Kandy. The Dutch (Protestants) persecuted the Catholics and the remaining Portuguese settlers but left Buddhists, Hindus, and Muslims alone. The Dutch levied far heavier taxes on the people than the Portuguese. Some migrants married Sinhalese women and their decedents are known as "Burgers". Many Dutch words migrated to the Singhalese language which is still in everyday use.

The Dutch referred to the island as " Ceylon" which was a derivative of the Portuguese "Sielen" derived from the Arabic "Serendib" referring to Rubies and pearls.

The British

Concerned that the French may control the Netherlands and therefore gain control over Ceylon, the British signed the "Treaty of Amiens" with the Dutch to transfer the occupied areas of the island to the British in 1802 and Ceylon became a crown colony. A year later they tried to invade the Kingdom of Kandy but were unsuccessful. But in 1815 they defeated the Kandyan king Rajasinghe II and finally ended the independence of the island.

After the third successful third Kandyan war and the Uva Rebellion, the British stripped Kandyan peasantry of their lands by the Crown Lands Ordinance No. 12 of 1840. They found that the uplands of Sri Lanka were very suitable for coffee, tea, and rubber cultivation. By the mid-19th century, Ceylon tea had become a staple of the British market bringing great wealth to a small number of British tea planters.

The planters imported large numbers of Tamil workers as indentured laborers from south India to work the estates since local Sinhalese refused to work for the British. Tamils soon made up 10% of the island's population.

The British colonial administration favored the semi-European Burghers, certain high-caste Sinhalese, and the Tamils who were mainly concentrated to the north of the country. Nevertheless, the British also introduced democratic elements to Sri Lanka for the first time in its history and the Burghers were given a degree of self-government as early as 1833. It was not until 1909 that constitutional development began, with a partly elected assembly. Not until 1920 the elected members outnumbered official appointees. Universal suffrage was introduced in 1931 over the protests of the Sinhalese, Tamil, and Burgher elites who objected to the common people being allowed to vote.

However, the credit goes to the British for introducing coffee, cinnamon, rubber, tea, etc. building roads and railway systems and English was designated as the official language and Colombo the capital. Finally, Sri Lanka gained independence in 1948.

Another positive side to the European invasions was the Catholic Schools built by missionaries in Sri Lanka including St, Anthony's College in Kandy which I was fortunate to attend, which eventually led to the opportunity to go to Japan.

My desire to go to University and graduate as an Engineer did not work out. Instead, I followed an alternative path as a trainee in the Irrigation Department and was assigned to a project in the north of Sri Lanka. My job involved a fair amount of traveling to my worksites which enabled me to fulfill my first wish of owning a car.

Father in his youth owned a business manufacturing and marketing radios, but his ill health due to over work he had to abandon it. However, he continued to invent and build electronic devices as a hobby at home in the workshop he built at the back of the house.

As a teenager, I was fascinated by my father's hobby and got deeply involved in his projects. Since I spent all of my free time after school and at the weekends on these projects in the workshop, I was excused from regular day-to-day chores. My mother nicknamed the workshop the "lazy room". Father bought books on radios, electronics, and TVs for me to learn, even though at that time there was no TV service in Sri Lanka. This experience encouraged me to think about my future in technology and decided to work my way to achieving my dream job of working in an engineering Development Lab inventing new things and perhaps patenting my ideas.

As luck would have it an opportunity arose to go back to college for further education in the UK in Mechanical and Electrical Engineering. I asked my parents if they would support me. Since our parents always supported us with anything to do with the education they agreed to help me even though it was financially difficult.

Arriving in England.

I arrived in England in 1962 and completed my College degree in 1965 and found my first dream job as a Development Engineer based on my degree and experience in electronics working with my father in the Industrial Instruments division of Smiths Industries company in London. So, my second wish to work in a development lab was accomplished. My third wish to marry someone outside of my race also came true at this lab when I met Barb my future partner in life.

My next job was in a company in London specializing in Electronic equipment Crossfield Electronics for the graphic arts and the printing industry as a Senior Development Engineer, during which time I, along with two friends decided to drive the 9000-mile journey through 21 countries overland by car from London to Colombo. A book based on the journey has been published in paperback and e-format on Amazon Kindle Publishing. After the trip, I came back to the UK and got married to Barb, and have two wonderful children.

I got my next dream job in September 1973 when I was offered employment in an international Development Laboratory in Welwyn Garden City which lead to our move to Japan.

Kiri Amarakoon

Chapter 1

Why were we in Japan?

In the 1980s I was employed as Senior Development Engineer by a research organization known as Rank Xerox Development Laboratory (RXDL) in the UK. The company was a joint venture between Rank Organization in the UK and Xerox Corporation in the USA, a world leader in document creation and marketing with over 100,000 employees worldwide. The partnership was called Rank Xerox (RX). Xerox Corporation also partnered with a prominent photographic company in Japan called Fuji Photo. The partnership was known as Fuji Xerox (FX).

In 1982 Xerox Corporation decided to market a newly developed copier machine by Fuji Xerox and wanted to integrate a Recirculating Document Handler ("RDH") as an enhancement that we were developing at RXDL. They concluded that for an efficient transfer of technology a resident engineer knowledgeable about document handlers was needed in Japan. Since I was the manager of the team leading the development of the document handlers, I was offered the position which I accepted wholeheartedly as it has always been my desire to visit other countries.

I had to confirm that my family felt the same way as I did about another move since we had already moved house three times within the United Kingdom. Another move, especially another country, and moving back might be a tough idea to sell. I came home to my family and broke the news and said,

"I have been chosen as a candidate for a resident engineer in Japan. How do you feel about all of us moving to Japan for a few years"?

My wife Barb did not hesitate in deciding as she has always known that I loved to move about the world and learn different languages and the children being so young, she thought the experience would be beneficial in the years to come. So, to my delight she said.

"Yes, if that is what you want we will go"

It was just after Christmas when we told our 8-year-old son and 5 years old daughter. Christmas was still fresh in our daughter's mind so her first question was.

"Will father Christmas know I am in Japan"

Our reply was.

"yes of course he will"

And started planning our next move.

Getting the family ready to move to Japan.

At that time, we were living in a small town called Letchworth Garden City, Hertfordshire in the south of England about 30 miles north of London. Garden cities were designed with the environment in mind.

Both our children attended a private school called Sherradswood. Clare was in the Montessori class from the time she was 3 years old. Lee was 5 years old was also transferred to Sherradswood. Barb took them to school and picked them up on her push bike after school. I usually took them to school in the morning on my way to work.

Moving to Japan was not an easy task due to several complications.

Even though I was employed by the company in the UK, I had to be transferred into the US Corporation as a US employee as my salary was paid in US dollars and deposited in a bank in the USA. I had to obtain a US Social Security Number to pay taxes on my earnings in the USA. Fortunately, these were all arranged by the International Personnel Department in the USA

To obtain resident visas for Japan we had to get police reports, fingerprint records, and other security documents. We accomplish these at the local police office and the Japanese Embassy.

Since we would be in Japan for a few years, we had to find rental accommodation and schools for the children in Tokyo.

There were many other arrangements such as shipping our personal belongings and furniture etc. from our house to the accommodation in Japan. Shipping arrangements were also taken care of by the company

We had to decide what to do with the house in the UK while we were away. The options were to close the house up or rent it out. Renting meant that we would have to pay part of the rent for the house in Japan. The law in the UK was that, if you rent your house and wanted to return later, the renters cannot be forced out if they did not want to leave. With that in mind, we decided to close the house. The company arranged for heaters for the house and paid the utility bills. Barb's parents dropped by occasionally to check on other things and mow the lawn.

Our first trip to Japan.

To accomplish some of the above, we were asked to visit Japan to familiarize ourselves with the country and to find accommodation, select schools for our children, open bank accounts to find out about a car for our use, etc. All the expenses were paid by the company. On Jan 6, 1983, for the first time in our lives, Barb and I went to Japan and were looking forward to the new experience.

Tokyo has two international airports, one is Haneda serving the Greater Tokyo area and handled all the international and domestic flights until 1978. In 1979 a second new airport called Narita International Airport was commissioned to handle all the international flights to overcome the capacity and noise issues associated with Haneda Airport due to its proximity to a densely populated area known as Tokyo Bay.

Narita city is located approximately 30 miles (50 Km) east of Tokyo in the Chiba prefecture on the main Honshu island. Originally an agricultural region producing rice, peanuts (groundnuts), sweet potatoes, and other vegetables, Narita developed as a temple town dating back to 1603 in the Edo period. Millions of Buddhist pilgrims visit the temples yearly, generating an extensive tourist industry.

To build the Narita International Airport in 1966 in the eastern part of Sanrizuka, the government purchased a large area of farmland. This action provoked dissent among the farmers, leading to political disputes that delayed the opening of the airport from its completion in 1973 until 1978.

In 1983 there were no direct flights from London to Tokyo as it was not permitted to fly over Russia due to the cold war. The flights from London to Tokyo were via Anchorage in Alaska. The flight from London to Anchorage was around 10 hours with a stay over in Anchorage airport for several hours to change aircraft for the onward flight to Tokyo. The flight from Anchorage to Narita airport was about 8 hours. So, in total it took a whole day to fly from London to Tokyo.

We were in the business class section with no smoking permitted but some passengers ignored that rule.

We fly arrived at Narita Airport and had no idea how to proceed to our hotel in Tokyo. We followed the other passengers and arrived at Customs and Immigration. The Immigration officers were very courteous and after our passports and visas were checked we were allowed to enter Japan for 30 days. We found our way to the baggage area and collect our bags and went through customs. Since all we had was our clothes there was no hold-up there either. We inquired as to what options we had to get to Tokyo and were informed that there was an Airport bus that would take us to our hotel in Tokyo.

The bus was called Airport Limousine and the tickets were about USD 20. The route to Tokyo was through the countryside with terraced rice fields and what looked like a temple far away on a mountain. As we got close to Tokyo we went over an interesting bridge. The bus traveled through a business district with high-rise office buildings. It was an interesting journey. The bus took us to the Hilton Hotel in Akasaka in central Tokyo. Recently it was renamed Hotel Tokyu.

The head office of the Japanese partner Fuji Xerox, my future employer was a walking distance from the hotel. The subway station nearby was called Kokai-Gijido mae. Meaning near or in front of the Diet, the parliament building.

The Hilton was a modern hotel with a large entrance hall, a lounge, and comfortable rooms. There was a small restaurant for quick breakfasts and lunches and a larger restaurant in the basement for formal dining.

In the rooms, there were Japanese dressing gowns for relaxing called Yukata, chocolates, a coffee maker, and a complimentary bottle of whisky. After dinner, we got into our yukatas. This was a new experience for us. When we came back to the UK we brought some with us for wearing in the evening and after a shower.

The next morning, one of the US residents in Japan whom I had met in England, dropped by the hotel to brief us on what we needed to do during our stay in Japan such as choosing schools, finding suitable accommodation close to schools, opening a bank account, etc.

Later that day, a Japanese gentleman came to meet us to guide us around the schools, where teaching was done in English generally known as International Schools. He naturally assumed that we were from America and that we would choose ASIJ (American School in Japan) which followed closely the American curriculum and was located in a town called Shinjuku which the children of residents from the USA attended. We explained to him that ASIJ was the wrong school for our children as we are from the UK and the US curriculum would not be beneficial to our children. We would also prefer a school with a "Montessori" class for our daughter so that she can continue her experience in a Montessori school she had in the UK and for our son a boy's school in the same area.

The gentleman was confused as he was not prepared for this complication. He called someone on the phone to confirm that it was ok to visit other schools. After the call, he suggested that we look at schools in the suburbs of Tokyo. But, as per his instructions, we had to have a look at ASIJ first. After that, we were taken to a couple of other International schools around Tokyo and finally to a girls' school called Seisen, in a suburb called Setagaya, which had a Montessori class. As luck would have it Seisen had an associated boy's school nearby called St. Mary's, with a free school bus to take children from Seisen to St Mary's, which was perfectly suited for our son.

This was ideal for us since it enabled us to take both children to Seisen in the morning and our son could take the bus to St Mary's. So, we chose the two schools. It so happened that the Montessori teacher at Seisen was a Sri Lankan lady called Miss Perera.

The next thing we had to do was to find accommodation that was convenient for the schools and access to the expressway for me to go to work in Ebina.

The company used a real-estate agency called Ken Corporation. The next day an agent who spoke perfect English from the agency came to the hotel and picked us up. We explained to him that we had already selected our schools in Setagaya and would like accommodation in the vicinity. He showed us several apartments nearby Setagaya where other US residents were renting. They were quite a way from the schools and we were not happy living in an apartment.

Finally, he took us to a house that was still under construction in Setagaya nearby the schools we chose. In Japan the side roads did not have names, they were identified by the area. Unlike other countries we were familiar with, the houses were not numbered in the sequence along the streets, they were assigned in the sequence they were built.

The address of the house we were taken to was 8-13-30 Fukazawa, Setagaya Ku. This means the house was in the 8th Chome pronounced "Cho-may" Japanese character 丁目, meaning postal district, in the the13th block house number 30, in the town of Fukazawa in Setagaya ward of Tokyo. The areas of Tokyo and its suburbs are divided into Wards called a "Ku", a Ja Japanese character 区.

The address is written in Japanese = 東京都世田谷区新町 8 丁目 13−30.

To identify each district and area, the details are marked on lamp posts. So, to find an address one would look for the nearest lamp post.

The owner of the houses that we were shown belonged to a gentleman called Ai-san who inherited from his parents a large plot of land compared to typical plots of land for houses around Tokyo. He took the opportunity to remodel his house into three separate houses two of which were intended for rent. He occupied the last house furthest away from the road and built it as a typical Japanese house with tatami mat flooring etc. More about typical Japanese houses to follow.

The two houses that were intended for renting were designed similarly to an American style. We were shown both houses and found that they were similar in size and layout. A paved area in front of the first house was parking to comply with the requirements to own a vehicle away from the narrow roads. Since the front house was nearest to the busy and noisy road, we opted to take the middle house.

The House

The house had four bedrooms, a large lounge, a dining room, and a large kitchen. The entrance to the house we chose was on the side of the building accessed by a paved pathway from the road. Next to the entrance was a mailbox on a stand with a screen for writing the name of the occupants. To the left of the entrance was a heat pump for heating and cooling.

The entry door was a wide brown double door leading up to a small hallway. As in all Japanese houses, the entry door was about 10 inches below the house floor. As is the Japanese custom, this is intended for removing shoes before entering the house. Slippers are usually placed by the entrance for the visitor's use if they chose to do so.

To the right of the entrance was a flight of stairs leading to the upper floor. From the hallway, a pair of glass paneled doors led into the large lounge with windows facing the back garden. To the right of the lounge through a pair of glass paneled sliding doors was the dining room with a patio door to the small back garden. To the right of the dining room through a pair of glass paneled sliding doors was a large kitchen with a breakfast bar. Typical American appliances such as a large fridge, an oven with a cooktop, a dishwasher, a sink, and cupboards. An unusual feature was a box built below the floor with a lid for cold storage which Barb used to store baking tins.

The upper floor had four bedrooms with walk-in wardrobes. The main bedroom had its bathroom and the other bedrooms share a second bathroom.

The streets in the suburbs are very narrow and usually, one-way The street where the house was located was a narrow one-way street from the main highway route # 246 named "Tamagawa Dori" which ran below the elevated expressway called "Shuto Kōsoku-dōro", meaning "Metropolitan Expressway" central Tokyo.

Even though our street was narrow and one-way, it was also a bus route. Nearby amenities within walking distance of the house were, the "Sakurashinmachi" railway station, "Komazawa" Olympic park, and a grocery shop called Summit. Opposite the house was a kindergarten school. It seemed this house was perfect for us, so we said yes please we would like to rent this house.

We were then informed that as the construction of the house was not complete yet and as we were the first inhabitants could we please choose the carpets, curtains, and other final finishes to the house? So, Barb and I made suggestions and they continued to get the house ready for our arrival.

During the next few days in Japan and we opened a bank account with the Japanese branch of the American bank called Marine Midland where my salary would be deposited in Rochester, NY, USA. On January 19th after two weeks of a wonderful experience, we left Japan and headed back to the UK via Sri Lanka for a couple of days to visit our family and arrived in the UK on January 23rd, 1983.

Barb's response after the trip.

"I must admit it was difficult dealing with packing the house contents as I was on my own, Kiri having started his new job. After our "look-see" trip we decided to take most of our household items, including furniture as we were leaving our house in the UK empty and not renting it out. Sorting what I thought we would need and trying to anticipate future needs took most of my time. My goal was to try and keep things as close to what the children were familiar with in the way of food whilst living in Japan so inevitably I stocked up on familiar items ready for shipment. Marmite to name but one."

Further preparations for the move

Having selected a house and schools we came back to the UK from our first trip to Japan. Then, the company asked us to visit the Head Office in Stamford, Connecticut, USA for a briefing to finalize the job and other personal details. On February 14th we flew to Hartford Connecticut Airport and took an airport shuttle to Stamford. We were met by the Senior

Second visit to Japan

However, when we returned home from our visit to the USA, I had to make a second trip to Japan to meet the Japanese team and familiarize myself with their plant in Ebina where I would be working. Which meant that Barb had to take care of the moving preparations on her own.

My ticket was booked for the 17th Feb 83, two days after the trip to the USA. I decided to rent a car for use during my visit and got a voucher for $ 1000.00 US dollars from the Hertz car rental company even though I was advised against it as it would be impossible to find my way around as most of the road signs and maps were only in Japanese.

Similar to our previous trip, after a nearl20-hour-long plane journey via Anchorage, Alaska, I arrived at Narita airport very tired. The customs and Immigration took quite a while. I had a reservation as before at the Hilton Hotel in Akasaka. I took the Airport Express train to Tokyo and a taxi from the station to the hotel.

Renting a car to drive to the office in Ebina.

The next morning, I was ready to rent a car with a $1000 voucher for the Hertz car rental firm. After I had breakfast and got dressed went down to the reception desk. I handed the voucher to a couple of clerks at the reception desk and said.

"I would like to rent a car, could you please call the Hertz agent and order a small car."

Both clerks at the desk looked at the voucher and shook their heads and taking sharp intakes of breath in the customary Japanese way and said.

"Sir, we don't know how to handle this please wait a moment

This request was not something that they came across especially from foreign visitors. They called the manager and showed it to him and the Manager had the same reaction. Then they realized that there was a Hertz agent from the USA staying at the hotel and said.

"Sir, please wait a moment we have an agent from Hertz staying here, we will call him down perhaps he can help."

They called the agent who came down to the reception desk. I explained the situation and showed him the voucher and he said

"Not many people who come on business trips rent a car in Japan as it is difficult to manage the roads and maps. But if you want to hire a car I can find an agent nearby and get you a car."

He asked the receptionist to call an agent who rented Hertz cars and after nearly two hours of waiting, someone brought a nice Subaru car to the Hotel and handed the keys to me.

There was a small newsagent shop in the foyer of the Hotel, I asked them if they had any maps of the Tokyo and Ebina area in English, and they said no and that all the maps they had were only in Japanese. I had no choice so I bought some maps covering Tokyo and the Ebina area.

I asked the shop assistant a few questions about driving down to Ebina. He directed me to the expressways and I thanked him and got into the car waiting outside the hotel. I was able to find the shut expressway from the hotel and drove west to get to the Expressway called the Tomei to drive to Ebina. The expressways took me almost to a town called Atsugi near Ebina. From there I took some country roads past some fields and found Ebina town.

I found my way to the office by enquiring at a gas station in Ebina town. At the office gate, I informed the guard that I was there to meet an Engineer called Takeuchi-san. A few minutes later someone came and I was escorted to the visitor parking lot. He then took me to the office and I was introduced to my group Manager, Sakamoto-san, and section Manager Kobayashi -san. I was assigned a desk next to Sakamoto-san and a secretary called Suzuki-san who spoke excellent English.

The office was a large open room with desks arranged in lines. Some Engineers had drawing boards next to the desk. Not even the group Manager had a partition for privacy. He sat by the back wall away from the windows near the entry door.

The rest of the day I spent time with the Engineers and was shown around the labs and the machine I would be working on. A free canteen lunch was provided by the company for all employees, but a couple of Engineers took me to a restaurant for my first all-Japanese lunch.

First real Japanese Restaurant.

After we sat at a table the waiter brought us small hot damp towels, and I was informed that the towels are a Japanese custom to clean hands before having the meal.

The meal started with a small brown bowl of soup called "miso" with seaweed (wakame), tofu, green onions, etc. "miso" is a traditional Japanese seasoning made from soybeans with salt, rice, barley, seaweed, etc. Miso soup consists of miso paste in a broth called "dashi" made from dried baby sardines, shavings of dried and smoked tuna, dried shiitake mushrooms, etc. Miso soup is a side dish usually consumed with the main meal.

Our main meal was called "ramen" a noodle dish consisting of 'ramen noodles'. In a savory broth consisting of soy sauce, salt, miso, and (tonkatsu) pork bones, a topping of seaweed, spring onions, bamboo shoots, and other ingredients. Ramen is one of present-day Japan's absolute favorite delicacies, costing very little and being widely available in restaurants and ramen bars on almost every street corner in towns.

To eat the meal a pair of "chopsticks" were provided. The soup bowl is moved to a side and is consumed with the meal using a Japanese porcelain soup spoon.

To eat Japanese food, you have to learn how to use the traditional Japanese eating implement called chopsticks, a pair of equal-length wooden sticks about 8 to 10 inches long tapered at one end.

They can be made from wood, bamboo, metal, ivory, ceramics, etc. They are usually held in the right hand secured by fingers to pick up food. When not in use they are placed on the rest. They are also used as cooking utensils. They were first used by the Chinese dating back to 1200 BCE. Later they spread to East Asian cultures including Japan, Korea, Vietnam, and other south Asian countries.

I enjoyed the meal very much and the company of the hosts. One of them asked me.

" How do you feel about coming over to Japan"

To which I replied.

" I feel very lucky and honored to be asked"

During the rest of my visit, I spent time with the Engineers and was shown around the labs to familiarize myself with the machine. While I was there I met a couple of Xerox residents working at Ebina.

The next hurdle for me on the first day of my visit to Ebina was getting back to my Hotel in Tokyo. Even though getting there was quite straightforward, getting back turned out to be a nightmare. Once I got to Tokyo there were many one-way systems and my Japanese map was not much help. After getting lost several times I eventually managed to find my way to the hotel quite late for dinner but that did not detract me from driving around Tokyo and going to Ebina for the rest of my stay in Japan. I flew back to England on February 24th to get ready to move permanently to Japan a week later on March 5th, 1983.

Chapter 2

Geography and History of Japan.

Now would be a good time to describe the details of the makeup of the country of Japan and its history.

Geography

Japan consists of five main islands.

HOKKAIDO annexed to Japan in 1869 is the northernmost island and is the second largest with a population of around five million. It is characterized by a cool climate, vast plains, and forests.

HONSHU is the largest island with around one hundred million inhabitants and the center of economic and political power. Most of the population is concentrated along the south edge of the island known as the "Pacific Belt" running along the Pacific Ocean. The northern region is mainly rural with mountains and fishing areas along the Sea of Japan. The second large commercial and industrial complexes centered are around Osaka and Kobe. The cultural centers are around Nara and Kyoto within Honshu.

SHIKOKU Is a smaller rural island with around four million inhabitants. A sparsely populated mountainous region is located on the southern coast of the Pacific Ocean with fishing as its major economic activity.

KYUSHU is the third-largest island located to the south of Honshu with around thirteen million inhabitants. The climate is subtropical due to its southern location. The industry is agricultural products such as rice, tea, tobacco, sweet potatoes, and soy. The largest city is Fukuoka. It has the most active volcano in Japan, known as Mt. *Aso*, and hot springs.

OKINAWA is the fifth major island roughly 400 miles from Kyushu with around 1.2 million inhabitants. It was a strategic location during world war two under the control of US troops. Currently, there are several US bases.

There are several smaller islands around mainland Japan.

Early History of Japan

Kofun era

The earliest documented era of Japan was from 250 to 538 CE, known as Kofun with the introduction of "Shinto", which is the worship of gods was the earliest widespread religion. The rituals practiced are the focus of Shinto was to guide the believer to a proper lifestyle ensuring connection to gods who came in many forms such as natural elements like forests. Eventually, they began to build shrines which are still thriving today.

Yaoi and Auska Periods

During the *Yaoi* period meaning "new life" around 300 CE rice farming and the use of iron, and bronze started. From 538 to 710 was known as the *Auska* period when Buddhism was introduced coexisting with the Shinto religion. The Buddhist Soga Clan took over the government around 580 BC and an article of constitution establishing social order was introduced, it was during this time the name Japan (Nippon) or Nihon meaning "land of the rising sun" was introduced hence the picture of the sun on their flag.

The first Kanji character means "sun" the second character means "origin" derived from the character for a tree, and the line at the bottom indicates the root.

日本

In 645 Soga clan was overthrown by the Fujiwara clan using ideas from the Chinese philosopher Confucius. All the land in Japan was nationalized and distributed equally among the farmers.

Nara Period

The next big change was the Nara period from 710 - 794 AD when a city based on the capital of China's Tang Dynasty was constructed. During this period Japan suffered many outbreaks of diseases and famines causing many deaths. In 794 AD the capital moved to modern Kyoto. The soldiers known as "Samurai" armies were mobilized in 1274 AD to confront the invasion by Kublai Khan of the Mongol empire.

Samurai soldiers in their amour

Shogun Period

The country continued to grow until the Shogun period around 1300 during the Kamakura period. Local area rulers were known as "daimyos". During the final century of the Ashikaga shogunate, the country descended into another more violent period of civil war which started in 1467. The daimyos took sides and burned Kyoto to the ground while battling for their preferred candidate. They fought among themselves for control of the country. One enduring symbol of this era was the ninja, who were skilled spies and assassins hired by *daimyōs*. Buddhist temples also raised their armies.

Sengoku Period. 1534- 1582

Oda Nobunaga was a daimyo and a leading figure of the period. He is regarded as the first "Great Unifier" of Japan. He was named "Demon King" due to his thirst for war. As the head of the powerful Oda clan, he fought wars against other daimyos to unify Japan and emerged as the most powerful daimyo overthrowing Ashikaga Shogunate in 1573. Conquered most of Honshu island by 1580, and defeated the *Ikkō-Ikkū* rebels, a group backed by Buddhist temples in the 1580s. Nobunaga's rule was noted for the brutal suppression of those who refused to yield to his demands. He was killed in 1580 when *Mitsuhide* ambushed him in Kyoto and forced him to commit seppuku, which is the act of stabbing oneself in the stomach.

Oda Nobunaga

Edo period 1600-1868

Few figures loom larger in Japanese history than *Tokugawa Ieyasu.* Born in a fractious Japan, where feudal lords regularly battled one another, Tokugawa rose to power and became known as one of the country's three "great unifiers," which helped to put an end to Japan's warring period. Following a decisive victory at the Battle of *Sekigahara* in 1600, the largest battle of the feudal era, Tokugawa was appointed *shōgun* — the military and political leader of Japan — by the Japanese emperor on March 24, 1603.

The new shōgun unified Japan under his leadership, ushering in a new era known as the Tokugawa period, lasting 250 years, also called the Edo period (the former name for Tokyo), is known for its relative peace, political stability, and isolation, as Tokugawa closed off mainland Japan from the rest of the world. Several movies have been made depicting this period.

Tokugawa

In 1853, the Tokugawa Shogunate's long reign began its decline when the Americans arrived in Edo Bay and introduced the reclusive island nation to modern naval technology. But thanks in part to its "great unifier," the country stepped into the future as a united nation.

Tokugawa was influenced by the Chinese "Confucianism" which led to the division of the society into four different classes to follow the samurai ideology called "bushido" meaning the way of life of the warrior. The order of hierarchy was: -

"Daimyo",
"Samurai",
Peasants,
Craftsmen
Merchants.

It was during this period that the practice of suicide called seppuku or *harakiri* was introduced. Apparently "*Samurai*" had so much power, they could kill a peasant for any reason and no questions asked.

Foreign trade and Christianity.

In 1543 a Portuguese trading ship was blown off course and landed on an island just south of Kyushu. They were the first Europeans to set foot in Japan. They introduced many European items including muzzle-loaded long guns known as muskets. The daimyos used around 300, 000 of these guns in their armies.

The Portuguese were allowed to trade and set up colonies which led to the introduction of Christianity by Francis Xavier in 1549. However later in 1564, the Buddhist clergy objected to this and destroyed the premises occupied by the Christians. Later followed a period of mass execution of Christian monks by the Japanese.

The Shogunate was weakening by the 18th century and the samurai had to find other jobs than being a warrior. People drew inspiration from books brought over by the Dutch, who were the next to arrive in Japan.

In 1853 a fleet of American ships arrived in Japan which led to turmoil as the US wanted to end Japan's isolationist policies. The shogunate had no defense against American gunboats and had to agree to permit trade with America. The Western countries imposed what became "unequal treaties on Japan stipulating that Japan must allow citizens from these countries to visit or reside on Japanese territory and allow imports and trade with Japan.

Chapter 3

Beginning of modern Japan.

Meiji Period 1868 - 1912

Finally, in 1868 the Tokugawa shogunate failed and the Satsuma domain convinced Emperor Meiji to call and end the Tokugawa shogunate the Meiji period continued from 1868 to 1912 led by Emperor.

The Meiji government started the modernization of Japan to achieve equality with Western powers. They abolished the Edo class structure and started a major development of the railway, telegraph education, banking, etc., adopted western clothing, and the calendar, and sponsored western science and medicine.

Taisho Period 1912- 1926

Taisho period with Emperor Taisho developed a more democratic government and grew as an International power. During World War I they sided with European Allies and seized Asian Colonies belonging to Germany.

Showa Period 1926-1989

Emperor Hirohito's sixty-year reign is the longest record in Japanese history. During the first twenty years rise of extreme nationalism and expansionist wars with China, Korea, and other countries led to America imposing economic sanctions against Japan. Japan reacted by allying with Germany.

Japanese Empire

Unfortunately, like the other world powers, Japan started to build an empire by invading countries in Asia. In 1941 Japanese Prime Minister and the army general *Tojo* decided to break the American embargo through military force. In December 1941 they launched a surprise attack on the American fleet at Pearl Harbor in Hawaii. They also invaded Asian colonies of the USA, UK, and Netherlands.

During this period the Japanese military was responsible for such war crimes as the mistreatment of prisoners of war, the massacre of civilians, use of chemical and biological weapons as depicted in films like Bridge on the River Kwai in Burma and Town like Alice during the Japanese invasion of Malaya in 1942. The Japanese military earned a reputation for fanaticism, often employing banzai charges meaning fighting almost to the last man against overwhelming odds. In 1944 the Imperial Japanese Navy began deploying squadrons of kamikaze pilots who crashed their planes into enemy ships. This is similar to the Japanese custom of committing suicide instead of living in shame called seppuku also known as Harakiri the practice dating back to the 17th century.

In 1945 Americans captured the Island of Saipan and began bombing major cities in Japan during the largest naval operation 150,000 soldiers and 150,000 in Okinawa died.

However Japanese would not give up and Americans realized that invading mainland Japan would lead to more and more casualties. Since America had no other alternative, they decided to use the newly developed Atomic Bomb. On August 6th, 1945 US dropped bombs on Hiroshima killing 70, 000 people, and a second bomb was dropped on Nagasaki killing another 40,000 people. The same year on August 9th Soviet Union declared war on Japan and invaded Manchuria.

Japan had no alternative but to surrender, on August 14th Emperor Hirohito communicated this to the world through a radio broadcast.

After the war America occupied Japan with General MacArthur running the country alongside Emperor Hirohito the military was disarmed and the Japanese colonies were given independence. Although the Japanese economy was in bad shape after the war, Japan soon grew by promoting manufacturing and technology.

By 1955, the Japanese economy had grown at an annual rate of 10%. The population increased and Japan became the second-largest economy after the USA. They dominated the Electronic and Automobile industry by 1985. That was the time we were fortunate to live and work in Japan. That concludes my brief history of Japan.

Back to our move to Japan.

Chapter 4

Moving the family to Japan

Finally, we were set to move house and family to Japan. Barb did a great job of organizing the move. A neighbor organized our trip to Japan via Sri Lanka and Singapore for the four of us within the budget allowed by the company.

We left the UK on the 5th of March and arrived at our family home in Sri Lanka and spent 4 days with the family. Flew out on the 10th to Singapore and stayed over a day in a nice hotel. Spent the day looking around the town and doing a bit of shopping. Bought a portable electronic organ for Lee and a Table cloth that Barb liked. The next day our flight was on Singapore Airlines and to our great delight we were upgraded to first-class seats, children loved the trip. During the flight, Lee was invited to visit the cockpit of the aircraft and chat with the Pilots. Arrived at Narita airport on the 12th morning and went through the complicated procedure at Customs and Immigration as we were coming over as residents.

We were booked at the Tokyo Hilton Hotel and had no difficulty getting there from the Airport since this was my third trip to Japan. We had to stay in the Hotel until our rented house was ready. We booked two rooms for the four of us. The children loved staying in the Hotel for a couple of weeks. When we went down for meals in one of the restaurants, Lee loved calling the waiters snapping his fingers, and ordering things.

There were quite a few shops on the ground floor. We had a good look around and ordered a few things. I ordered a new Sony TV, a stand and a VCR to be delivered to the house after we moved there, and Barb ordered a tea set she liked.

As residents, we were provided with a company car for our use during our residency. To select a car, we were asked to visit the company head office nearby in Akasaka. Barb and I walked to the office and were shown to a parking lot on the roof where there was a selection of Toyota and Nisan cars. We looked at them and chose the Nisan Laurel as it was a big luxury model suitable for our family. A couple of days later the car was delivered to our Hotel. The car had fancy knitted seat covers on all the seat back and headrests. In the trunk, there were four tire chains in a box for use in the winter and an emergency reflective triangle. It seems that in Japan, as soon as there is an inch or so of snow on the road people install tire chains which ruins the roads.

Now that we got our car, we did a few trips around Tokyo and waited to hear from the Real-estate company to let us know when the house was ready.

Moving into our new home.

A couple of weeks later we were informed that the house was ready but our furniture etc. shipped from the UK was not delivered yet. Fortunately, we had an air shipment of essentials. A few days later our furniture and other household goods were delivered to the house. So, we all got into our new car and drove down to Setagaya to our new home.

We unpacked our belongings and started to set up the house for a long stay. Hung the curtains that Barb had packed from our house in the UK and made the house comfortable.

Lee and Clare had their rooms and we had the main bedroom. The spare room was prepared for guests. During the next days, we registered Lee and Clare in their schools and I got ready to go to my work while Barb continued to set the kitchen up and rooms making the house comfortable and homely.

My morning drive to work from the parking space in front of the house was along narrow one-way streets to route 246 (*Tamagawa Dori*) which leads to the Tomei Expressway heading south-west to Atsugi the nearest big city to Ebina where my office was. From the Atsugi toll gate, the drive was along local roads passing rice fields and arriving at the small town of Ebina. Occasionally on my way to work, I took the children and dropped them off at Clare's *Seisen* school, from there Lee took the school bus to his school St. Mary's.

Tomei expressway goes along the countryside with tea gardens and other agricultural suburbs. It is a busy highway and even though my journey was only 36 miles, due to daily traffic jams it can sometimes take 2 hours to complete the journey. The return journey home was a lot worse than the morning commute. As I recall, once it took me 2 hours to drive 2 miles from the Tomei toll gate to Setagaya.

The whole country is covered with expressways, most of which are toll roads. Several expressways cover the northern and eastern parts of the country. Greater Tokyo Area has an elevated toll expressway that goes around the center of the city called "*Shuto Kōsoku-dōro*", meaning "Metropolitan Expressway", "*shuto*" also means "capital city". Operated and maintained by the Metropolitan Expressway Company Limited.

Chapter 5

Working in Japan.

On my first day, I arrived at the company gate and was shown to a parking lot within the office compound designated for Foreign Residents working in Japan. The local employees' parking lot was across the road from the compound.

The office complex consisted of two five-story buildings for use by the research departments situated to the left of the entry driveway. The large building on the right was one of the manufacturing buildings connected to the research building with an overhead walkway. Within the research building, different departments occupied different floors. The mid-volume printers and copiers development group which I was part of was on the third floor. I arrived at my desk at the back of the office near the wall separating the office from the corridor and was welcomed by the manager Sakamoto-san and the secretary Suzuki-san.

The group I was working in had around 15 engineers and designers and 4 young girls as secretaries. The group occupied a large room about 100 feet long parallel to the corridor and 60 feet deep up to the windows from the central corridor. Engineers were assigned a desk, a chair, and a low filing cabinet next to the desk. Two desks were placed back to back for two workers facing each other, On top of the desk at the back were thick folders for filing their work, they acted as a separator between the two engineers facing each other. The designers were assigned a drawing board and a desk. It was a completely open plan with desks separated about two feet from each other. Even the managers did not have separate rooms as offices unlike in the UK. It was more like a classroom.

A custom practiced in most work environments in Japan was, for employees to go through a warm-up routine before starting their day's work. My work was mainly writing reports and communicating between the development team back in the UK and the Japanese development team resolving any questions each team may have.

The employees had free access to stationery for their work and to refreshing drinks such as green tea and miso soup any time from two machines installed by the elevators. The lunch break was an hour at noon announced by a siren. A subsidized lunch was provided to employees in a canteen in a nearby building with a fixed menu. A second a canteen where a variety of meals can be ordered from a menu at reasonable prices. Most of the foreign residents preferred that faculty.

At the official finishing time of 5 PM, I left work and battled my way back home to Tokyo. Sometimes the traffic jams lasted for miles and it could take three to four hours to drive the 36 miles home.

Working with Japanese Engineers.

Most of my interactions were with four or five engineers. They were, the planning team leader - design team leader, electrical design team leader, Software team leader and group manager, and of course my secretary.

We discussed any changes that needed to be done to the document handler that was being developed at Welwyn Garden City Development lab in the UK. It was my responsibility to communicate this to the team back in the UK. The time difference between the two countries meant that during Japanese working hours it was nighttime in the UK. So, all our communications were done via regular mail or phone calls as email was not in common use at that time.

Lunchtime was announced at noon and most of the team went to the company canteen for lunch. I was not so keen on the company lunch so I brought sandwiches for lunch and got a free cup of green tea to wash it down with. The group reassembled after lunch around 1:00 PM and got back to work.

Private Room

On Friday, after work at 5:00 PM, it was customary for some members of the group to go out to a local restaurant for a drink and a meal, occasionally I joined them. We went to traditional Japanese restaurants with separate private rooms for groups of customers. The floor of the rooms was raised about a foot above the corridors. In the room was a typical low dining table and cushions around it to sit down on. Sometimes underneath the table, there was sort of a dugout for people to drop their feet down while sitting on cushions on the floor. Sometimes, the seats had a backrest like a normal chair.

On the table, there were small bottles of sake, Japanese rice wine, and small cups called *Sakazuki* nick named *Ochoko* by each of the seats. After sitting down, as is Japanese etiquette, the person sitting next to you picks up the sake bottle and fills your small cup. Then it is your turn to fill the sake cup of the person next to you. Also, on the table were warm damp towels at each seat to clean our hands and ready to eat. Sometimes there are dishes of "Edamame" which are raw soybean pods that are not ripe.

A waitress dressed in a kimono came in and knelt by the sliding door and asked what would we like to order in Japanese of course. One member of the group ordered several bottles of beer and a meal to follow. The meal generally starts with miso soup followed by noodles in a bowl known as "Ramon". Sometimes the meal is cooked at the table on a portable gas burner with several vegetables, fish, and slices of beef which you cook yourself by putting in each item at a time known as "sukiyaki". More about Japanese food later.

Just before New Year's Day, the whole group of about 50 of us went down to the "*Izu*" peninsula for a celebration party. I was invited to join. It was a big ryokan or a minshuku where we stayed overnight, I shared a room with one of the engineers. The hotel had a large room where the dinner was served on low tables and we were sitting on the floor on cushions as usual. There was a stage at one end of the room. Each team was required to perform a play on the stage during the dinner. My team created a sketch referring to the program we were working on which was called Super Bulldog. It so happened that there was a popular sauce called " Bulldog " in Japan and I was asked to have a one-line part in it. The manager was the lead and he said in Japanese to me: -

"Kiri-san, Bulldog wa do desuka?"

This means "what do you think about our machine Super Bulldog?"

As a response, I pulled out a bottle of the sauce that Suzuki-san gave me from my jacket and said my line in Japanese, which was: -

" Sakamoto-san, so-su mitai desu ne"

Meaning "sounds like a sauce" for which we got a good laugh and applause. The electrical group team performed a play mimicking a child being born, which was a bit crude but got a lot of applause and cheers.

As part of doing business, Japanese workers organize similar large parties when they have foreign visitors. One such party I remember was when several people came over from the USA research labs. That was held in a similar large restaurant with a stage where each of us had to sing a song using a karaoke machine.

I learned a Japanese Karaoke song from a tape I was given called "My name"

After the singing session we were shown how rice cake "*mochi*" was made by pounding soaked white rice in a large wooden " and a pestle" the pestle is a large wooden hammer with a long handle. We all had to go pounding the rice and made rice cakes and ate them with lunch.

I continued to enjoy my work in Japan. Towards the end of the first year, a new Engineer first name Akira joined the group who had been a resident a couple of times in the USA and spoke excellent English. He had a very nice young secretary and he offered to share her with me since my previous secretary was busy with other duties. We still keep in touch with each other regularly and visits our home whenever he comes over to the USA.

Tokyo Business show.

Tokyo business show is a yearly event held in a large Convention center in Tokyo. This particular event is participated by major technology-based industries such Xerox, Canon etc. The purpose is to display the capabilities of their current and future products to convince customers why they should buy their products.

I visited the show with my secretary and one of the US residents from USA. It was a nice summer day in May 1984. It was very informative and the Xerox both was very busy with interested customers,

After my residency in Japan, the group organized a big party and we were given a Japanese picture as a parting gift. I wish it was a longer time in Japan than a year and a half.

Managers invitations to their homes

My team manager and the group manger invited our family to visit their homes for the day.

Group manager Sakamoto-san's house was not far from our home in Setagaya so we went for the day for lunch. His wife and children welcomed us cordially and we were shown around his typically Japanese house and sat down for lunch. After our lunch they gave us a picture as a gift.

Executive Director Kobayashi-san's house on the other hand was in the countryside quite a long away from Tokyo we had to take the highspeed bullet train called "Kodama" from Tokyo main railway station to Odawara. Kodama Shinkansen is a slower bullet train that serves local stations and generally stops at every station along the Shikansen, the highspeed Shinkansen on the other hand only stops at few major stations. and take a local train to a station near his house. He came and picked us up at the station and we drove to his big house in the countryside with rice fields and woods. The exact location of his house not mentioned here due to privacy reasons.

Shinkansen-新幹線

Shinkansen means -"New Main Line' and generally known as the "Bullet Train" relating to the shape of the front speed at which it travels up to 260 km/h or 160 mph. future proposed speeds are as high as 500km/h. To achieve these speeds the tracks had to be specially laid down with welded joints to avoid noise. The trains are also fitted with an extensive array of safety devices such as the Crash avoidance system, automatic braking systems, earthquake detection systems etc. They have an impressive safety record over the 50 years of operation,

Lee by the Shinkansen

It has a very high reputation for time keeping so much so the stopping time at a station is just 3 minutes, during which time the passengers have to board the train,

Seating in the carriages are like airline seats with head including a head rest cloth. The seats can be turned around by 360 degrees so the passengers can sit facing each other. The train travelled through beautiful countryside with neat tea plantations on the mountains and rice fields in the rural areas.

Children enjoying the day

From Odawara station we took a local Odakyu line train to heading north for a few miles to a station near his house. He came and picked us up at the station and we drove to his big house in the countryside with rice fields and woods. The exact location of his house not mentioned here due to privacy reasons.

Inside the house

The exterior of his house looked very much like a modern two-story western house rather than a Japanese house which can be seen in the background in the picture. However inside of the house was a typical Japanese house with many artifacts and tatami mats on the floor.

We spent the day with the family, Clare and Lee went out with their son and enjoyed the day in the fields and a stream. We had a typical Japanese lunch sitting on the floor around a low table seen in the picture.

Wooden slippers "*Geta*"

After lunch Kobayashi -san took us to a famous temple nearby called Daiyuzan Saijo-ji Temple is located in South Ashigara City up in the mountains of Kanagawa Prefecture. The temple is surrounded by rich mountainous nature.

One key element in this temple is a large collection of traditional Japanese wooden slippers called "*geta*". Children had a great time climbing on these slippers of varying sizes.

There were many visitors and several Buddhist and Shinto monks at the temple. We spent several hours and went back to Kobayashi-san's house and in the evening returned to our home in Setagaya. It was a great day out.

Other residents from the USA in Japan

There were eight of them some seen in the picture when we went to a business/vacation session in one of the resorts in the Izu Peninsula.

One of them Chuck came to Japan about 6 months after we settled down. They also decided to live away from downtown Tokyo and moved to an apartment in a town called *Den-en-chofu* not far from us in Setagaya. It was one of the apartments we looked at but did not suit us as it was far away from the children's schools and too small for the four of us. Chuck liked the Nisan Laurel car we selected and he picked the same model.

They became very good friends of ours and treated our children as their own. We visited each other and went to several public festivals known as "matsuri" around Tokyo. They visited us after we came back to the UK for a week or two. We visited them when they came back to the USA for about three weeks and drove down to Florida to his sister's house in a Recreation Vehicle we had many problems on the way. But it enables us to take our children to Disney Land in Florida. We still keep in touch since we moved to the USA.

Dave was the senior resident and all the others were part of the low-volume groups. I was the only one representing the mid-volume group.

We used to get together regularly at each other's hoof with the residents. For Christmas they organized a big party at the Tokyo American Club, the party ended with people making speeches and singing songs. Our son Lee was never shy about performing at gatherings, he made a speech and played a silent night on his portable electronic organ.

After we moved to the USA, we continually have resident gatherings at each of our houses in turn. Unfortunately, some of them have passed away.

Chapter 6

Barb's experiences in Japan.

While Kiri was at work and the children were at school, I was left alone at home but had to deal with many new things that cropped up in our lives living in Japan. One of them was to pick up Clare and Lee from Clare's school Seisen which is about half a mile away. I walked to the school and walked back home with the Children.

The location of our rented western-style house was perfect. It was within walking distance of the school, supermarket, train station, and a wonderful park that we went to often. We had quite a few immediate expenses when we arrived as our electrical items needed to remain in the U.K. as the voltage was different in Japan. Kiri purchased television and later video equipment. I found myself avidly watching the advertising between programs trying to work out what was being promoted. In the end at the supermarket, I resorted to unscrewing the tops of containers and smelling! This was my first experience of being illiterate.

Japanese housewives shop daily arriving at the supermarket on their bicycles wearing their aprons. My routine in the UK was to plan several meals and buy in advance and I found the small quantities very limiting. Fortunately, the supermarket was just a short walk and I had plenty of time, the only limitation being the amount I could carry back home. The "trolley" or baskets are very small as are some of the items. Bread for instance was a uniform shape, square cut into about six slices. On one memorable occasion when Kiri's brother was visiting he offered to go and buy some butter. I had described the container.... black and white cows, yellow colored packaging. He came back with cheese!! The other "foreign" mothers at the school were very helpful and if one of us purchased the wrong thing, a "beware" was filtered through so we could avoid it and not waste money. Who would have thought you could buy a pack of half-boiled eggs?? Being illiterate was not easy.

After a short while and getting to know the staff at Clare's school, I was approached and asked if I would teach an English conversation class with Japanese women who had lived outside of Japan and knew a little English. I was very hesitant to accept as I have no experience teaching. The woman I would be replacing was an American who I later found out did most of the talking in the class which I thought defeated the object. Teaching English in Japan can be very lucrative but I did not want any payment as I didn't have a clue how to approach this and if a fee is given, I thought you should at least expect some professional standard.

The group of ladies in the class varied each week but on average seven would attend. I took props from home (Clare's toy telephone) and created scenarios for them to practice their English with each other. They were at first very shy and didn't even know each other's first names even though they knew each other. I remember when we were about to leave for the U.K. I invited the ladies for a Sri Lankan meal. I was astonished at how many came, all probably interested in the type of food. They came armed with fruit and just like women all over the world, headed for the kitchen and started to prepare what they had brought with them. They were quite amazed that it was a healthy meal!

Barb's English class

Our neighbors in the front house were from Australia and had three children. Friendships formed very quickly and I think made time in Japan more enjoyable, especially for our children. Having planned to leave the UK, I had thought about Christmas and so was somewhat prepared. We hosted Christmas lunch, and Clare helped me make the traditional "crackers" with gifts and paper hats (saved and brought from the UK) the sorted into paper tubes and decorated and never went "bang" unlike the shop-bought ones in the UK. All five children enacted a small play for entertainment. On occasion, I looked after the youngest child, Meredith who was about two years old. She was a sweet girl and as I had a bicycle with a pillion seat, I was able to take her with me when it was time to collect Lee and Clare from school. I can't recall how long this went on for eventually she had, a Japanese nanny which I was pleased about as I was then able to enjoy my free time a little more.

I attended *Ikebana* (flower arrangement) classes and learned how to cover a tea chest with the material. The tea chest is wooden on the outside and the inside is lined with metal. Women in Japan use them for storing clothes. We purchased and shipped at least six tea chests, gave away three to family members and I covered three with fabric that we still use.

I did attempt to learn Japanese but on the occasions that I spoke and asked a question the reply was always in English. Also, being what the Japanese called a "native" English speaker, conversation in English was always preferred.

I thought it important to get the children involved in something after school so I volunteered to run the Boy Scouts of America group at Lee's all-boys school. Clare, unfortunately, did not want to join the Brownies at her school, she was still very shy and only five. She did join in with the activities Scouts did, coming on hikes, etc. I sometimes found it difficult to think of craft projects that would appeal to all the boys but I am pleased I had that experience and I hoped it helped Lee to be more confident in making friends although the Australian neighbor's son was "the favorite".

During the school holidays, I did take the children to the cinema and the zoo. It was a challenge back then as direction signs were not in both languages. I would stand, underground train map in hand, and attempt to match up the kanji characters to try and find our destination and which line to take. We saw the first Star Wars film in Tokyo and it was a relief to see that the dialogue was in English with Japanese subtitles. It would have been a disaster had it been the other way around.

The many trips on the underground system made us familiar with our local station, decorated with pink tiles. The station before was green and before that yellow so we knew when our station was approaching. The public transport system was and probably still is very safe and clean. We all felt very safe and relaxed when out in public and fact, our children and our neighbor's children frequently went on bike rides together around the neighborhood. They loved to go to the "10 yen" shop and buy sweets. They always took change with them to phone home if they had a problem....no mobile phones those days! That kind of freedom at their age was wonderful and would never have happened in the UK.

On one occasion I had to go and pay a telephone bill that was in arrears as we did not know we had to pay it since the company paid all our bills. So, Kiri asked me if I could find the telephone office and pay the bill while he was away at work. By this time, we all had push bikes. I took the bill and some maps which were all in Japanese and got on my bike and went looking for the office to pay the bill. I have no idea I managed to do it since there were no road names on any of the roads and no house numbers. I followed the information on lamp posts and eventually found the office and paid the bill.

During our relatively short time in Japan, we went on several trips and saw a quite a bit of the country. I encouraged the children to keep scrapbooks with booklets etc. of the places we visited. Not long after we arrived we visited the recently opened Disneyworld. It would become one of many trips there. We did have a memorable trip to Hong Kong with an American couple to buy a computer and a cheap Apple copy. I think we all had culture shock there as it is so different from polite and considerate Japan.

At that time in Japan, credit cards and cheques were not used when purchasing large items. This would mean that a large amount of cash was withdrawn from the bank "in case" it was needed. We never felt vulnerable carrying this amount of money.

Chapter 7

Children's life in Japan

Our son was 8 years old and our daughter was 5 years old when we moved to Japan. They both were excited at the prospect of traveling to a new country. As mentioned earlier Clare's only worry was whether Father Christmas would know to deliver her presents to Japan.

Lee with his trophy

Having had new experiences at that young age such as visiting Thailand, and Singapore and traveling in first class on the areophane was just the beginning for them. They enjoyed their stay in a luxury hotel for a couple of weeks in Tokyo until our new house was ready. When we moved into the house they had their separate rooms so that they could enjoy personal things like toys and desks for studying.

Clare with class mates

Another curious custom in Japan was that everything has a season for buying. We bought two desks for our children during the "Desk season". We brought them back with us and gave them away when our children got older.

When they were registered at their schools they found lots of things to do. Lee joined the boy scouts. Barb volunteered to run the meetings as she thought it was a good idea to get Lee involved in the "Pinewood of America" derby for which he had to build a car with the parts supplied by the school for which he received a trophy for coming first in the race.

Clare continued in the Montessori school and as luck would have it her class teacher was a nice Sri Lankan lady called Miss Perera. Clare participated in many extracurricular activities with girls from several countries.

Lee's school boy scouts organized a walk to Yokohama from Setagaya for the students and parents. Barb participated with Lee and Clare on the 18-mile 6-hour journey along country roads. They organized a bus for the home journey.

As Barb mentioned they had a wonderful time in Tokyo with their new bicycles going to a shop which they called ten-yen shop with new friends from Australia from the house next door. When we were shopping they came along with us and bought things they liked, such as video games and toys. They also accompanied us when we visited ancient temples such as Nikko, and Nara. And popular tourist attractions such as Izu and mount Fuji and had the experience of staying in a minshuku for a few days and hot springs. When Barb's parents and my mum and RB visited us in Japan they were able to join them on other trips.

Lee's experiences in Japan.

Lee was quite active at school and enjoyed going to Akihabara with me to electronic and game shops. We bought him handheld video games and a radio-controlled car which he loved playing with. He enjoyed judo classes and playing the electronic organ we bought in Singapore at parties and played father Christmas with our neighbor's children on Christmas day. He loved playing with his transformer toys which were quite popular at that time. Lee enjoyed our trips and played the big brother to Clare.

Summary of Clare's experience in Japan

Clare turned six years old and Lee turned nine years old when we were in Japan. Below is some of what Clare remembered in her own words.

I seem to recall our front door having some sort of cool ringtone or feature to it.

Our mailboxes were a light silver metal with ridges on them…and a flap that lifted had our names written on it. My neighbor's daughter Susan whom I became friendly with would leave letters there for each other in the boxes.

Riding bikes around Komazawa Olympic Park and eating pineapple-flavored ice lollypops from the small caravan vendor just next to the track. I'm pretty sure they were clear wrappers.

Fried chicken, thick logs of string cheese, and chewy squid are my most memorable food items.

I remember the kitchen had a cool hatch on the floor to store things.

Our fish tank was in the kitchen on a ledge. I think Lee's fish ate/attacked my fish, Angel.

The sounds of those barking small stuffed dogs and cats that do flip is all I remember of Takashimaya or any toy shop.

Flying those fish kites in that park. Which is the same park that we did our sports day in I think?

Jumping over the garden snake to go out into the back garden….and then jumping back over it to tell mum it was there.

I don't remember what my contribution was, but I recall Susan doing a puppet show for our Christmas dinner with her Japanese dolls with their arms on sticks.

Walking down to that corner restaurant with the spinning sign out front.

I only remember the deer at Nara mainly because of the photos…. but I think we stayed at a place that had a really large and wide dark wooden staircase.

I don't entirely remember how we got to school, but I think dad dropped us off…and I think Seisen was at the bottom of a hill and we took a left turn to get into it?

I remember the Seisen Bazaar….and a lot of baked goods. Pretty sure mum had a table of homemade treats.

I know I spilled the nail polish on my bedroom carpet…. but I only remember the disappointment from mum and dad. I'm pretty sure it was a bright pink or red color.

I remember Dolly Dolphin at Disney Park….and I think I had a lot of Disney characters…but mainly remember Donald Duck.

I remember picking Nanny &Granddad up from the airport…. but not the part welcoming them in the airport. I remember being on the top level of the car park loading the bags in the car and there being a warm wind and I didn't know what to say to them because I felt shy.

Mum doing Ikebana classes

I remember the light fitting in the dining room. I seem to recall it being on a chord that you could pull down and lift back up.

That long hike to Kamakura with mum and Lee's scouts' group. I just remember feeling quite good about myself at the time that I was doing it with the big kids.

That really cold outdoor pool at the Tokyo American Club.

I mainly remember the feeling of happiness from living in Japan. I'm sure Lee and I fought, but I don't remember them the way I do the ones in England and the US. I could be wrong, but it seems like we did more family outings and activities together over there. Maybe because all we had was each other. It does feel like we were there a lot longer than 1.5 years the way that we were so settled within our schools and home. I do wish I was a bit older when we were there so I could have appreciated the history and culture that you both introduced us to. Also wish I was older so that I could have been more of a friend to hang out with for mum instead of a nuisance causing her to chase me around tables and injure herself.

As throughout our whole life, you have both always gone above and beyond to never make us feel like we have missed out on anything and always created a warm and loving home wherever our little family unit ended up.

Chapter 8

Visiting ancient sites

Trip to Nikko (日光)

During one weekend we decided to make a trip to the ancient city of Nikko known for its temples and shrines. It was a two-hour drive from Tokyo. Four of us started early in the morning and headed north along what is known as the "Romantic Road" passing many interesting tourist attractions such as hot springs, volcanos waterfalls, and mountains. And of course, the world heritage sites of Nikko.

The entrance to the town was next to the National Park home of Japan's most decorated and famous *Toshogu* shrine, the magnificent memorial to Tokugawa Ieyasu, the founder of the Tokugawa Shogunate who ruled Japan for over 250 years until 1868, detailed in the Japanese history section earlier.

Toshogu Shrine

Ieyasu's remains are deposited at the shrine as the deity *Tosho Daigongen*, meaning "Great Deity of the East Shining Light". Initially, it was a relatively simple mausoleum. Later in the 17th century, his grandson enlarged it into a spectacular complex.

Nikko had been a center for Shinto and Buddhist worshipers for many centuries before Toshogu was built in the 1600s. The National Park consists of mountainous landscapes, lakes, waterfalls, hot springs, wild monkeys, and hiking trails.

We spent the whole day in the shrine complex. Children loved climbing the rocks and walking around various buildings. Unfortunately. I was busy with my new video camera and paid little attention to my family which I regret to this day.

Just beyond the entrance gate of the Shrine, there was a group of storehouses with many colorful and elaborate wood carvings including the most famous one of the wise monkeys depicting "see no evil, speak no evil, and hear no evil" this saying believed to have come from China in the 8th century. There were carvings of "elephants" that were carved by an artist who may have never seen elephants.

Three Wise Monkeys

The main shrine is a long building consisting of a praying hall, connected to the main hall which is dedicated to Ieyasu. Visitors are allowed in but no photographs were allowed.

There was a waterfall nearby called Kegon Falls considered to be a tourist attraction. So, we drove out of the Shrine along a winding road but when we go to the fall viewing stage it was so misty we could hear the fall but could not see it.

Visit the Izu Peninsula

We wanted to see the iconic Mount Fuji while we were in Japan. So, I asked one of the engineers Obara-san at the office (who was very knowledgeable about Japan). He often came up to my desk and talked about various aspects of Japan and encouraged me to learn the Japanese language and understand Japanese customs etc. As such he was the obvious person to ask about the best way to visit mount Fuji and experience local culture. He explained about traditional Japanese guest houses known as Ryokans and Minshuku sometimes called "pension". He suggested that we visit the Izu peninsula with hot springs and stay in a ryokan. And then made a call and reserved a ryokan in Atami on the Izu peninsula and a traditional hotel by lake Yamanaka with views of mount Fuji.

The hot springs of Atami have a long history dating back to the 1600s when shogun Tokugawa Ieyasu carried water from the hot springs back to his residence in Edo, now Tokyo.

We drove from our home in Setagaya along the coast stopping at several interesting places along the seaside like Hiratsuka beach so the children could have a little rest and go on the beach etc. We arrived in Atami city and found the ryokan that we booked and checked in. It was owned by a family who showed us around the facility and took us to our room. It had a hot communal bath fed from a hot spring known as an "onsen" and a communal dining room for breakfast and dinner.

Ryokan room

The room had tatami mats on the floor, a TV, Telephone, a small safe, and a low table with cushion seats around it. There were no beds but there was a cupboard that contained futons and pillows.

There were four dressing gowns called "*yukata*" for us. We had our dinner and got the futons out and went to sleep.

The next morning, we went down to the hot spring bath known as "*ofuro*", A typical bath contains a line of water taps about 15 inches above the floor and small low stools at each tap for bathers to sit down and clean themselves before going to the hot bath below ground level about 10ft by 10 ft and 15 inches deep. We all followed the procedure and got into the bathtub and enjoyed ourselves. After our bath, we got our yukata on and went for breakfast.

The breakfast room had low tables with cushions around them on the floor. A typical Japanese breakfast served consisted of: -

Bowls of rice, Miso soup and salad

piece of grilled fish,

Dish of pickles,

A raw egg and Tofu,

To eat breakfast, a pair of chopsticks and a soup spoon.

Cups of green tea.

After our breakfast, we left the ryokan and headed towards Mount Fuji where our next hotel was by lake Yamanaka. It was a modern hotel and we had two rooms. It was situated on an isolated piece of land with a sloping lawn towards the lake. I remember our children loved it and were playing on the lawn. Clare lay sideways and rolled down the incline while Lee was running after her. After we checked in we walked down to the lake and could see mount Fuji in the distance. We had a good night's sleep on proper beds and in the morning after breakfast, we checked out and drove to mount Fuji. There was a road heading up part of the mountain which we took and stopped at a little shop. It was cold and we spent a little time and headed down the mountain.

Most of the other trips were when Barb's parents and my mum visited Japan as described in the following sections.

Chapter 9

Family visits to Japan.

After we settled down in our house and got used to living in Japan, Barb's parents and my mother and brother came over for a visit. This allowed us to visit several interesting sites in ancient japan such as Buddhist Temples and Shrines. With my mother, we visited all the temples around Tokyo and the great Buddha statue in Kamakura.

Barb's parents came during the summer of 1983 for about three weeks. Clare and Lee were so excited and didn't stop talking to them as soon as they arrived at Narita Airport when went to pick them up. They were glad of the opportunity to visit Japan which was one of Barb's dad's wishes.

We treated them to lunch at the Tokyo American Club in Roppongi, Tokyo. Also took several trips to interesting places around Tokyo such as the Imperial Palace, Ginza famous for its shopping center and the " Kabuki-Za " theater, Akihabara, Hama gardens, and several temples and shrines

Imperial Palace

The Imperial Palace known as *Kōkyo* is located on the former site of Edo Castle, a large park area surrounded by moats and stone walls in the center of Tokyo. It is the residence of Japan's Imperial Family. Edo Castle used to be the seat of the Tokugawa shogun who ruled Japan from 1603 until 1867. In 1868, the shogunate was overthrown, and the country's capital and Imperial Residence were moved from Kyoto to Tokyo. In 1888 construction of a new Imperial Palace was completed. The palace was once destroyed during World War two, afterwards, it was rebuilt in the same style.

Akihabara

Akihabara (秋葉原), also called Akiba after a former local shrine, is a district in central Tokyo that is famous for its many electronics shops. On Sundays, Chuo Dori, the main street through the district is closed to traffic from 1:00 PM to 6:00 PM. And until 5:00 PM from October through March to enable shopping crowds to move freely.

The shopping area consists of hundreds of electronics shops. Larger ones such as Laox and Yodobashi Camera have several floors, each floor is dedicated to one type of electronic devices such as TVs, Computers, Video games, Audio equipment, Cameras, and components. Several smaller shops are selling one or two particular items such as electronic equipment like Oscilloscopes, Signal Generators, Power Supplies, etc. I still have an Oscilloscope and a power supply I bought in 1983.

I also bought an NEC desktop computer while we were in Japan, unfortunately, most of the software was in Japanese, so I sold it to one of the engineers in my office and bought an Apple II copy from Hong Kong.

Away from the main large shops, there are a couple of covered arcades where several one-man stalls specialize in a particular electronic component at reduced prices. I used to walk up and down these arcades and buy components I still have in my workshop. In addition to these, there were people selling parts of electronic assemblies discarded by the manufacturers outdoors along the sidewalk. I looked forward to the weekends when I used to go to Akihabara just to look around. Occasionally, I took our son Lee along to show him around the shops and bought hand-held video games.

Hama Rikyu Gardens

Tokyo has an ancient landscape garden in central Tokyo called "Hama Rikyu" (浜離宮), Located alongside Tokyo Bay featuring several seawater ponds which change level with the tides, and a teahouse on an island where visitors can rest and enjoy the scenery. The traditionally styled garden stands in stark contrast to the skyscrapers visible in downtown Tokyo.

The garden has served many purposes over the centuries. It was originally built as a feudal lord's Tokyo residence and duck hunting in the grounds during the Edo Period (1603-1867) but later served as a strolling garden and as an imperial detached palace before eventually being opened to the public in its current form. There are several ways to visit the gardens, we drove there and took our lunch with us. It was a very hot day but we all enjoyed the trip. From the garden, we walked up to Tokyo Bay where it was cooler.

Wooden bridges are serving as walkways between islands and the tea house on the pond. Clare was so excited in the garden she was running back and forth on one of the bridges and slipped and fell and was crying.

Chapter 10

Visiting Nara

Our next trip was an extended visit to the ancient city and shrines of Nara dating back to years 710 to 794 called the Nara period when the Capital of japan was Kyoto, as described in the brief history of Japan previously.

Before we visited Nara, I asked my colleagues at my office to recommend places we should visit and a hotel for our stay in Nara and the unanimous response was.

"Old Hotel Nara is the best hotel you will enjoy"

I called and booked three double rooms for Barb's parents, Clare and Lee, and Barb and me. It was expensive but worth it. I took two weeks off from my work and together with Barb's parents, Barb, Lee, and Clare loaded up our car and set out for our long drive to Nara from Setagaya, Tokyo.

The first leg of the journey was along the Tomei Expressway along the coast to Nagoya. We took it slowly and stopped at Shizuoka and Okazaki and several other rest stops. Visited Nagoya Castle and had our packed lunch.

Nagoya Castle was built by the "Owari Domain" ruled by Shogun Tokugawa Iyesu in 1612 during the Edo period on the site of an earlier castle of the Oda clan in the Sengoku period.

Nagoya Castle

Nagoya Castle was the heart of one of the most important castle towns in Japan, Nagoya Castle was destroyed in 1945 during the bombing of Nagoya in World War II and the reconstruction and repair of the castle has undergone since 1957. The castle has also historically been nicknamed for its famous

Onigawara(金鯱城), featuring "Golden Fish". Unlike ancient buildings in Sri Lanka made of stone, Japanese buildings were all made of wood. From Nagoya, we drove to the Hotel along some beautiful country roads and arrived in the evening.

Nara Hotel was a five-star hotel located on the hillside overlooking Nara Park. Opened on October 17, 1909, one of the most historic hotels in Japan was designed by Tatsuno Kingo the designer of the Bank of Japan building and the Marunouchi building of Tokyo Station. In 2009 the first centennial anniversary of the hotel was celebrated. Barb's mum was so impressed by the lobby and the stairs, she said

Nara Hotel Lee and Clare

"It is like the movie "Gone with the Wind" house".

Various heads of state, members of royal families, heads of government, politicians, actors, artists, and other notable persons have stayed at the hotel such as

Albert Einstein, a Swiss physicist.

Jawaharlal Nehru, Indian prime minister, and his daughter Indira Gandhi.

14th Dalai Lama, Tibetan spiritual head.

Lee and Clare in the deer

The next morning after a good night's rest we walked from the hotel past the *Ukimido* bridge towards Nara Park and the ancient temples and shrines.

Nara Park is a large park in central Nara. Established in 1880, location of many of Nara's main attractions including *Kasuga* Tisha Shinto shrine, and the Nara National Museum.

The shrine is famous for its hundreds of bronze lanterns donated by worshipers hanging from the buildings and many stone lanterns line its approaches. They are only lit twice a year during two Lantern Festivals, in early February and mid-August.

The park is also home to hundreds of deer freely roaming and grazing who were not afraid of humans and let them feed and touch them. Lee and Clare were excited and the deer let them touch and feed them.

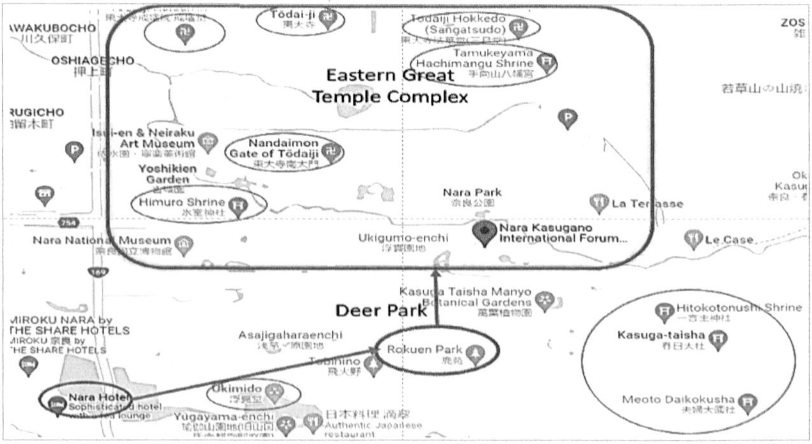

Visiting the ancient temple complex

Temples and Shrines

Note: -Throughout Japan, there are some 80,000 Buddhist Temples or Ministries and around 100,000 Shinto Shrines that are considered famous. Buddhism and Shintoism are practiced side by side, unlike believers of other religions. Included here is a just sample of ancient monuments. As it would be impossible to include all the important sites of worship.

Another UNESCO World Heritage Buddhist temple complex known as *Enryaku-ji* was built in 788 on top of mount *Hiei* north of Kyoto. It was later destroyed by Daimyo Oda Nobunaga in 1571 to put down *Hieizan* warrior monks occupying the Temple complex to oppose the ruthless behavior of Nobunaga. The complex was rebuilt later.

The first major recorded major Shinto shrine is known as Kitano *Tenmangu* and is located northwest of to. It is the first of 12,000 spiritual places dedicated to Tenjin in honor of Sugawara no *Michizane* (845–903), the famous scholar, poet, and politician of the Heian period. *Ten* means sky and *jin* mean god or deity. The original meaning of Tenjin, the sky a deity, is almost the same as that of Raijin (a god of thunder). The shrine is adjoining the *Kamishichiken* Geisha district and is famous for its tea ceremony performed by Maiko (trainee Geisha) in February, under 1,500 plum trees in bloom.

The shogunates or leaders of Japan made it a priority to update and rebuild Buddhist temples. The Japanese word for a Buddhist monastery is *tera* (寺) or Ji depending on kanji reading known as *Kun* or "*on*". So, the temple names frequently end in *-dera* or -ji. Such famous temples as *Kiyomizu-Dera*, Enryaku-ji, and *Kōtoku-in* are temples that use the described naming pattern.

Buddhist temples co-exist with Shinto shrines and both share the basic features of traditional architecture. Both *Torii* and *Rōmon* mark the entrance to a shrine as well as temples although torii is associated with Shinto and *Romon* is associated with Buddhism. Some shrines, for example, *Iwashimizu Hachiman-gū*, have a Buddhist-style main gate called *sōmon.* Many temples have a *temizuya* and *komainu,* like a shrine. These are described below. Conversely, some shrines make use of incense or have a *shōrō* bell tower. Others, for example, *Tanzan* Shrine in Nara – may even have a pagoda.

Temizuya

A temizuya is a tank of water in a shed provided for worshipers to cleanse themselves by washing hands and faces etc. before entering the temples or shrines. When we visited the temples we always used these to wash our hands.

Temizuya

Torri and Komainu

A torii (鳥居,) is a traditional Japanese gate most found at the entrance of or within a Shinto shrine, where it symbolically marks the transition from the regular common environment to the sacred space. A "torii" at the entrance usually indicates an entrance to a Shinto shrine, a torii icon can be found on Japanese road maps to show the locations of a shrine.

The first appearance of torii gates in Japan according to written history was during the "Heian" period around 922. The oldest existing stone torii was built in the 12th century and belongs to a shrine in Yamagata prefecture.

Torii gates were traditionally made from wood or stone, but today they can be also made of reinforced concrete, copper, stainless steel, or other materials. They are usually either unpainted or painted bright red with a black upper lintel.

Torri gate and Komainu

Origin of Torii.

There is some indication that the torii may be derived from the Indian word *Torana* which means a gateway, the Japanese characters can be translated as "bird perch". Some believe Japanese Torii existed before *toranas* in India.

Ancient Indian Torana sacred gateway architecture has influenced gateway architecture across Asia, especially as Buddhism migrated from India. Chinese gateways are known as "*paifang*". They can be found in Korea, Vietnam, and Thailand. The Elaborate Toranas can be found in India at the entrance to Hindu and Buddhist temples or shrines, or a city.

Komainu

Komainu is a statue of animals placed in front of the Tori Gate. meant to ward off evil spirits, modern komainu statues usually are almost identical, but one has the mouth open, the other closed However, exceptions exist, where both komainu have their mouth either open or closed. An example of one type of Komainu is shown in the picture, there are many shapes and sizes seen in Japan. They resemble guardian lion status found in temples in China and are believed to have originated from the Tang Dynasty. They can be found in India, Korea, and other eastern countries where Buddhism is practiced.

Similarities between temples and shrines are also functional. Like a shrine, a Buddhist temple is not primarily a place of worship: its most important buildings are used for the safekeeping of sacred objects (the *honzon*, a Japanese statue of sitting buddha equivalent to a shrine's shintai) and are not accessible to worshipers.

Unlike a Christian church, a temple is also a monastery. There are specialized buildings for certain rites, but these are usually open only to a limited number of participants.

Mass Religious gatherings do not take place with regularity as with Christian religions, and in any event, are not held inside the temple. If many people are involved in a ceremony, it will assume a festive character and will be held outdoors. The architectural elements of a Buddhist temple are meant to embody the themes and teachings of Buddhism.

The reason for the structural resemblances between the Buddhist temples and Shinto shrines lies in their common history. When Shintoism first encountered Buddhism, it became more interpretive as it did not try to explain the universe. A temple may look like a shrine, and obvious differences in architecture between them are few, often only a specialist can see them. Many visitors visit Buddhist temples and Shinto shrines for similar reasons such as prayer and luck. The two religions coexist due to their increased popularity of them.

Shrines enshrining local kami existed long before the arrival of Buddhism, but they consisted either of demarcated land areas without any buildings or of temporary shrines, erected when needed. With the arrival of Buddhism in Japan in the 6th century, shrines were subjected to its influence and adopted both the concept of permanent structures and the architecture of Buddhist temples. The temple names 'Ji" (寺) indicates it is a Buddhist temple rather that a Shinto shrine.

Horyu-Ji temple with Barb's parents

Horyu-ji

temple is considered to be the world's oldest wooden building founded in year 607 and designated a world heritage site in 1993.

Toda-ji (東大寺) Temple

We spent a whole day enjoying the vast Buddhist Temple complex known as "Toda-ji" which means the "Eastern 東 Great temple that was once one of the powerful Seven Great Temples, located in the city of Nara. It was originally founded in the year 738 CE, and opened in the year 752 CE. There have been several reconstructions since then, significantly the Great Buddha Hall(大仏殿 *Daibutsuden*) in 1709 which houses the world's largest bronze statue of the Buddha known in Japanese as "*Daibutsu*" (大仏).

The temple is a listed UNESCO World Heritage Site as one of the "Historic Monuments of Ancient Nara", together with seven other sites including temples, shrines, and places in the city of Nara.

According to records kept by Tōdai-ji, thousands of people helped construct the Great Buddha and its Hall. some 350,000 working directly on the statue's construction.

Sizes as displayed in the temple:

Height: 14.98 m (49 ft 2 in)
Face: 5.33 m (17 ft 6 in)
Eyes: 1.02 m (3 ft 4 in)
Nose: 0.5 m (1 ft 8 in)
Ears: 2.54 m (8 ft 4 in)

Great Buddha

The statue's shoulders are 28 meters across and there are 960 six curls atop its head. Buddha's golden halo is 27 m (87 ft) in diameter with 16 images each 2.4 m (8 ft) tall, consisting of eight castings, the head, and neck cast together as a separate element.

Unfortunately, a decline of the began as the center of power in Japanese Buddhism shifted away from Nara to Kamakura when the political power in Japan moved from the emperor's capital to the "*shogun*'s" base in Kamakura in the aftermath of the national civil war(1180–1185) between two clans during the late-"Heian" period. Tōdai-ji's role in maintaining authority declined. In later generations, despite repeated attempts to revive it; thus, no more ordination ceremonies take place at "Tōdai-ji".

Yakushiji One of Japan's oldest temples was constructed by Emperor *Tenmu* in the late 7th century for the recovery of the emperors. It has a strictly symmetric layout, with the main hall and lecture hall standing on a central axis, flanked by two pagodas.

Tōshōdai-ji

The temple was the biggest in Nara city Nara and was founded in 759 by the Tang dynasty Chinese monk *Jianzhen* during the Nara period. He was hired by the newly empowered clans to travel in search of funding from private aristocrats as well. The Buddhist temple of the *Risshū* sect in the city of Nara consists of Classic Golden Hall, also known as the *kondō*, which has a single-story, hipped tiled roof with a seven-bay wide facade. It is considered the archetype of "classical style". UNESCO has designated it as a World Heritage Site "Historic Monuments of Ancient Nara".

After visiting the temples etc., we took the children to Nara amusement park which was deserted since it was a really hot day. But the children did not care they had a great time. We all enjoyed the trip and headed back home. Barb's parents spent the rest of their stay doing things like visiting Komazawa Park, Takashimaya department, and Oriental bazaar shop which has various things from several countries like China, Korea, etc.

Second family visit.

My mother came over with my brother RB and his wife in April 1984 for about six weeks. Mother was a practicing Buddhist and as such, she wished to visit Temples and Shinto Shrines. We visited quite a few temples and shrines around Tokyo and the great bronze Buddha statue in Kamakura. When the Nara period declined due to civil war the center of Buddhism moved to Kamakura under the rule Minamoto shogunate in 1192.

Bronze Great Buddha

The current bronze statue was preceded by a giant wooden Buddha, which was completed in 1243 after ten years of continuous work which was damaged by a storm in 1248, along with the hall containing it. To replace it, a bronze statue was commissioned, and a huge amount of money was necessary for this and a new hall was raised for the project. At one time, the bronze statue was gilded. Traces of gold leaf can be seen near the ears of the statue. The new hall was also destroyed by a storm in 1334 and 1369 and was rebuilt but the new building housing the statue was washed away in the tsunami as a result of an earthquake in 1498. Since then, the Great Buddha has stood in the open air. Which was the one we saw as seen in the photograph. The statue is almost as big as the bronze statue in Nara Toda-ji temple.

Clare and Lee enjoyed their company and they were happy for the opportunity to visit□

Chapter 11

Houses, behavior, Language, clothing, Food, etc.

Exterior of houses

Traditional Japanese house

In contrast to houses in most countries, typical Japanese houses occupied by most of the population other than the wealthy people are small and compact. They are usually constructed with wood. Some of the houses date back 100s of years and look as if the wood was never painted or treated in any way However, modern houses in the countryside with space for a garden are full of character. Also built with wood and typically has beautiful gardens and unique interiors. Seen here is a traditional house built in the 1920s showing the garden and the corridor along the back.

Interior of Houses

The entrance hall is called "*genkan*" where people remove their shoes. The internal house floor is higher to prevent dampness from entering the living area. After removal, shoes are put in the "getabako"—a cabinet that derives its name from geta, wooden clogs, once commonly worn by Japanese people.

Entrance hall

Japanese rooms

A room called (和室, *washitsu*) which is used for many purposes has a unique interior design with tatami mats as flooring, they are also known as tatami rooms. They date back to the *Muromachi* Period (1338- 1573) when they originally served as study rooms for the wealthy before gradually becoming more commonplace as reception and living quarters.

Tatami mats are thick, woven straw mats that measure about one by two meters in size. Originally a luxury that only the wealthy could afford, tatami gradually became more common and can now be found in virtually all traditional Japanese homes. Tatami mats have been so integral to Japanese homes, that the size of rooms in Japan are commonly measured by the number of mats that would fit it, e.g. an 8-mat room. All footwear including slippers should be removed before stepping onto the tatami.

Tatami room and sliding

Sliding doors called *Fusuma* are made up of wooden frames covered in thick, opaque paper. The doors are typically used between adjoining rooms akin to large removable walls, allowing one to partition off areas or open up space as needed. Historically, fusuma have been the canvas

Another type of sliding door or partition is shoji, which is made up of wooden lattices covered in a translucent paper called washi. They are typically found along the perimeter of the building, allowing light to filter in. Some shoji doors incorporate sliding panels that move up and down like small windows to allow light or air to enter the room. Occasionally shoji may have a sheet of glass covering one side of the door. The Tatami mats and panels are renewed by craftsmen regularly.

Dining area

The dining area in a traditional home is just another room with a low table with cushions around to sit on the floor. Sometimes the tables have a built-in heater under the table and a blanket to keep legs and feet warm called a "*Kotatsu*". The whole family is seated around the table. We brought back one which we use when we have visitors.

Family dining table with blanket

In early traditional houses, the cooking was done in a room that had s sunken fire pit and the cooking pots were suspended above the fire pit and adjustable hooks as seen in the picture.

Sunken fire pit with pot hanger

Alcove (tokonoma)

They are recessed alcoves and are typically decorated by a hanging scroll in addition to a vase or flower arrangement. The decorations are typically changed to reflect the season. Traditionally, the most important guest is seated in front of the tokonoma.

Sometimes shelves, next to the alcove are built-in shelves for displaying decorations like vases and incense burners.

Ceilings

There are a variety of ceiling types in traditional Japanese-style rooms. In general, the ceiling is flat and simple, but in rooms such as a lord's reception hall or a temple's worship hall, the ceilings may be raised and decorated with paintings.

Movable Furniture

Folding screens are portable and are arranged in a zigzag fashion for the panels to stand without support. Free-standing partitions, called single panels are supported by legs. They are available in varying sizes to divide up a room for privacy and reduce drafts. Some expensive partitions are containing celebrated paintings. Other movable furniture such as lamps, mirrors for ladies' use for makeup, and small low tables were common items in a room.

A folding screen "*Byobu* "

Bedrooms

Traditional Japanese-style rooms are still very prevalent around Japan in ryokans and minshukus-type hotels similar to the one we stayed in on our trip to Izu discussed and seen earlier. The bedroom is a room with tatami mats with a built-in cupboard for storing items such as *futons* and pillows.

Futons are traditional Japanese mattresses that are laid directly on the tatami flooring. They are kept folded in the closet during the day and set out in the evening after dinner. We brought some back and still use them when we have visitors.

Chapter 12

About Japanese people

Japan is a unique country compared to some 30 countries I have traveled to for business and pleasure. Even today Japan is different from the countries I have lived in for long periods like Sri Lanka, the UK, and the USA. It was more so when we were fortunate enough to live and work in Japan back in the 1980s. The behavior of the people, the food, and the transport systems were highly disciplined. Before I go any further, it would be a good idea to give a brief history of this unique country.

Japanese Behavior

Here is a quick look at the major behavioral differences between people in Japan. Don Maloney wrote a book "Japan: It's Not All Raw Fish" when he was a resident in Japan as a light-hearted newspaper column for the Japan Times.

Some of these behaviors date back to the Samurai era and "Bushido". When we were in Japan in 1983 and 1984, some of the unique behaviors we observed.

How courteous the people were to one another when they met. They would bow their heads down to show respect. This custom date back to the 15th century during the "Daimyo" period.

Exchanging business cards when meeting a new person and say " Hagimemashite" meaning "nice to meet you". It means "this is the first time (meeting you)"

People would never cross the road at a pedestrian crossing until the sign says to cross even if there is no traffic on the road.

It is considered bad behavior to consume food or drink while walking along.

Most people are well dressed and well behaved.

They don't like to be embarrassed if they could not understand you and would avoid the situation by keeping away. For example, shop assistants will walk away if you did not speak to them in Japanese. So, I learned to say "Eigo o hanashimasu ka? "Meaning "do you speak English?" And many more.

Learning Japanese.

I am fascinated by all languages which began when I was young as my father spoke three languages, Sinhalese, Tamil, and English. He started to teach us Tamil t home, which I enjoyed, and was able to talk to my friends at college. So, when we were in Japan the company paid for Barb and me to learn Japanese using a visiting tutor it was an opportunity that I could not ignore.

I looked around and found a lady who came to our house once a week to teach us. Later on, two young students came to teach us spoken Japanese. They recommended several books which I still have. I also continued to learn the language on my own and bought several other books as I wanted to learn Kanji: -

Intensive Spoken Japanese Books 1 and 2
An Introduction to Modern Japanese
Practical Japanese
2001 Kanji
New Dictionary of Kanji Usage
Japanese Kana Work Book.
Japanese English dictionary

I still have these and use them as reference books and continued learning after I came back to the UK and later to the USA. There were Japanese classes at our office which I attended. I try to speak Japanese whenever I have an opportunity such as talking to my friend Miyazaki -san on Skype.

Japanese Language (日本語),

Pronounced "*Nihon-go*" meaning Japan Language spoken by about 128 million people, primarily in Japan, and is the national language. It is a member of the Japonic languages that have been grouped with other language families such as Ainu, Austroasiatic, and Korean.

Little is known of the language's prehistory, or when it first appeared in Japan. Chinese documents from the 3rd century AD recorded a few Japanese words, but substantial texts did not appear until the 8th century. Then it was known as Old Japanese influence by the Chinese language on the vocabulary and phonology. Late Middle Japanese (1185–1600) included changes in features that brought it closer to the modern language and the appearance of European words. Following the end of Japan's self-imposed isolation in 1853, the flow of words from European languages increased significantly. In particular, English words. These words are known as 'loan words" Japanese is a difficult language to master, but, with little effort and practice it can be learned.

It has a pure vowel system of consonant length and a lexically significant pitch-accent, namely,

A, I, U, E, O -- Pronounced - Ah, Eee, Uu, Eh, Oo

The grammatical function of word order is normally subject–object–verb, with particles marking, and sentence structure is a topic–comment. Sentence-final particles are used to add emotional or emphatic impact, or make questions.

Nouns have no grammatical number or gender, and there are no articles. Verbs are conjugated, primarily for tense and voice, but not a person. Japanese adjectives are also conjugated. Japanese has a complex system of honorifics, (meaning expressing status or politeness) with verb forms and vocabulary to indicate the relative status of the speaker, the listener, and the persons mentioned.

Spoken Japanese does not seem to have any relationship with Chinese, but in written form, it makes use of Chinese characters, known as *kanji* (漢字) , and vocabulary borrowed from Chinese. The writing system uses modified Chinese kanji characters as well as "hiragana" and "katakana", Latin script is used in a limited fashion (such as for imported acronyms). The numeral system uses mostly Arabic numerals as well as traditional Chinese numerals.

Frequency of Characters.

Characters	Types	Proportion of corpus
Kanji	4476	41.38%
Hiragana	83	36.62%
Katakana	86	6.38%
Punctuation/symbols	99	13.09%
Arabic numerals	10	2.07%
Latin letters	52	0.46%

Kanji

Kanji characters are pictograms, meaning they are based on everyday articles and nature such as water, rivers, mountains, etc. The original characters were refined for today's use. Japanese Kanji evolved from Chines characters with simplified pictograms for ease of writing and reading. The word itself means "Chinese (or Han) characters." Early forms were first used in Japan as early as A.D. 800 and evolved slowly into the modern era, along with hiragana and katakana. Following Japan's defeat in World War II, the government adopted a series of rules designed to simplify the most common kanji characters to make them easier to learn.

Elementary school students have to learn about 1,000 characters and 2000 for high school. Beginning in the late 1900s, Japanese education officials have added more and more kanji to the curriculum. Because the language has such deep historical roots, literally thousands more kanji have evolved and are still in use.

Examples: -

English	Original	Final	Strokes	Pronunciation
Man		人	2	Hito
Above		上	3	Ue
Below		下	3	Shita
Water or liquid		水	4	Mizu
Rice field		田	5	Ta
Big		大	3	Oki
Small		小	3	Chisai
Woman		女	3	Onna

平仮名（ひらがな） hiragana

a	あ	安	i	い	以	u	う	宇	e	え	衣	o	お	於
ka	か	加	ki	き	幾	ku	く	久	ke	け	計	ko	こ	己
sa	さ	左	shi	し	之	su	す	寸	se	せ	世	so	そ	曽
ta	た	太	chi	ち	知	tsu	つ	川	te	て	天	to	と	止
na	な	奈	ni	に	仁	nu	ぬ	奴	ne	ね	祢	no	の	乃
ha	は	波	hi	ひ	比	fu	ふ	不	he	へ	部	ho	ほ	保
ma	ま	末	mi	み	美	mu	む	武	me	め	女	mo	も	毛
ya	や	也				yu	ゆ	由				yo	よ	与
ra	ら	良	ri	り	利	ru	る	留	re	れ	礼	ro	ろ	呂
wa	わ	和	wi	ゐ	為				we	ゑ	恵	wo	を	遠
												n	ん	无

Creation of Hiragana from Kanji

These basic characters are combined or extended to write more complicated words. For example: -The character for the East -- 東 is created by combining the character Sun 日 and Tree 木 to indicate the morning sun behind the tree. The character for the Forrest -- 森 is created by combining three trees -- 木

The capital Tokyo is a combination of kanji for the east 東 and capital 京 meaning the east capital. The old capital was Kyoto, Combination of Capitol 京 and Section 部

Tokyo -- 東京 Kyoto -- 京部

Here is a small sample of Kanji characters,

□

亜哀愛悪握圧扱安暗案以位依偉囲委威尉意慰易為 異移維緯胃衣違遺医井域育一壱逸稲芋印員

Japanese Alphabet

In addition to Kanji characters, there are two sets of alphabets namely Hiragana and Katakana. They are the first truly Japanese alphabet that originated in the 9th century when people wanted to create their writing system distinct from Kanji, borrowed from the Chinese. Together, they are known as the kana. In Japanese script, it is easy to differentiate Hiragana and Katakana from the complex Kanji. The three together make up the Japanese writing system.

Hiragana

Hiragana was originally called "*onnade*" or 'women's hand' as they were used mainly by women. Men wrote in kanji and katakana. By the 10th century, hiragana was used by everybody. The word hiragana means "ordinary syllabic script".

Below is the complete set of the Hiragana alphabet. The top line on the left table is the vowels. The right table shows the way to create additional sounds from basic Hiragana. For example, "ka" becomes "ga" by adding the strokes above the character Below each character is the English pronunciation of the character

Hiragana is used mainly for writing Japanese words to enhance the pronunciation of Kanji characters and to write words there are no Japanese Kanji characters available. For example

私は: "*Watashi*" - ha -- I and "ha" (the subject marker)

車を: "*kuruma*" - "wo" -- the car and "wo" (the object marker)

見た: "*mi*–" "ta" the verb “see” and "-ta" (marking the verb as past tense)

Japanese sentences are written from left to right and down the page, as seen below as well as

Basic hiragana syllables

あ a	い i	う u	え e	お o
か ka	き ki	く ku	け ke	こ ko
さ sa	し shi	す su	せ se	そ so
た ta	ち chi	つ tsu	て te	と to
な na	に ni	ぬ nu	ね ne	の no
は ha	ひ hi	ふ fu	へ he	ほ ho
ま ma	み mi	む mu	め me	も mo
や ya		ゆ yu		よ yo
ら ra	り ri	る ru	れ re	ろ ro
わ wa				を wo
ん n	ひらがな Hiragana			

Additional sounds

が ga	ぎ gi	ぐ gu	げ ge	ご go	平仮名
ざ za	じ ji	ず zu	ぜ ze	ぞ zo	
だ da	ぢ ji	づ zu	で de	ど do	
ば ba	び bi	ぶ bu	べ be	ぼ bo	
ぱ pa	ぴ pi	ぷ pu	ぺ pe	ぽ po	
きゃ kya	きゅ kyu	きょ kyo	ぎゃ gya	ぎゅ gyu	ぎょ gyo
にゃ nya	にゅ nyu	にょ nyo	ひゃ hya	ひゅ hyu	ひょ hyo
びゃ bya	びゅ byu	びょ byo	ぴゃ pya	ぴゅ pyu	ぴょ pyo
みゃ mya	みゅ myu	みょ myo	りゃ rya	りゅ ryu	りょ ryo
じゃ ja	じゅ ju	じぇ je	じょ jo	ちゃ cha	ちゅ chu
ちぇ che	ちょ cho	しゃ sha	しゅ shu	しぇ she	しょ sho

the right to left from each line down the page seen below.

Katakana

Katakana has a similar set of characters as Hiragana and is used mainly for writing foreign words.

The word katakana means "fragmentary kana," as the scripts are derived from components of the more complex Kanji. Katakana is used to write words borrowed from other languages, like *rokka* (locker), spun (spoon), *botoru* (bottle), *kohii* (coffee), and *te-buru (*table).

Unlike the Hiragana system (used for Japanese words the Kanji doesn't cover), the Katakana is used for foreign language transcription into Japanese and for loan words and to represent scientific-technical terms, and the names of minerals, animals, and plants. The names of most Japanese-owned companies are also written in Katakana.

Similar to Hiragana by adding two strokes above the basic character added sounds are created for example

Other sounds are created by adding a second character written smaller than the main character as seen below. Such as "kya", "kyu" and "kyo" as seen in the chart above.

Phonetic sign	a	ka	sa	ta	na	ha	ma	ya	ra	wa	n
Hiragana	あ	か	さ	た	な	は	ま	や	ら	わ	ん
Katakana	ア	カ	サ	タ	ナ	ハ	マ	ヤ	ラ	ワ	ン
Phonetic sign	i	ki	shi	chi	ni	hi	mi		ri		
Hiragana	い	き	し	ち	に	ひ	み		り		
Katakana	イ	キ	シ	チ	ニ	ヒ	ミ		リ		
Phonetic sign	u	ku	su	tsu	nu	fu	mu	yu	ru		
Hiragana	う	く	す	つ	ぬ	ふ	む	ゆ	る		
Katakana	ウ	ク	ス	ツ	ヌ	フ	ム	ユ	ル		
Phonetic sign	e	ke	se	te	ne	he	me		re		
Hiragana	え	け	せ	て	ね	へ	め		れ		
Katakana	エ	ケ	セ	テ	ネ	ヘ	メ		レ		
Phonetic sign	o	ko	so	to	no	ho	mo	yo	ro	o	
Hiragana	お	こ	そ	と	の	ほ	も	よ	ろ	を	
Katakana	オ	コ	ソ	ト	ノ	ホ	モ	ヨ	ロ	ヲ	

Complete set of Hiragana and Katakana characters

Japanese clothing

Kimono きもの/着物

The most famous and well-known clothing item is the "*kimono*" which means " item to wear" the literal translation of "*ki* " comes from the word "*kiru*" which is to wear on the shoulder and "mono" is an item.

It is a traditional Japanese garment and Japan's national dress. When worn, a kimono often indicates the wearer's age, gender, the formality of the occasion, and less commonly, their marital status. This extends to the decoration, how it is worn, and accessories as well.

Examples of Kimono

The kimono was considered daily wear by the Japanese people and dates back to the Kofun period (300 to 538 AD) believed to be introduced from China. The style and the culture changed according to the specific period.

During the "Heian" period (794-1185) it evolved into multi-layered kimono for women, colors that were used to represent ranks in court for men (the deeper the color, the higher the rank), also specific combinations of colored layers to represent the seasons and plants.

Construction of a kimono

During the "Edo" period (1603-1868), the sleeves of the kimono grew in length, and the "obi" (sash) migrated from a hidden tie into a longer and wider visible sash which needed its accessories to keep it in place. From this point onwards, the basic shape of the kimono has remained unchanged.

The kimono is a wrapped-front garment with square sleeves and a rectangular body and is worn left side and wrapped over the right. The kimono is traditionally worn with a broad sash, called an obi, and is commonly worn with accessories such as *zōri* sandals and *tabi* socks.

Kimonos have a set method of construction and are typically made from a long, narrow bolt of cloth. There are different types of kimonos for men, women, and children, varying based on the occasion, the season, the wearer's age, and – less commonly in the modern day – the wearer's marital status. Despite the kimono's reputation as a formal and difficult-to-wear garment, there are types of kimono suitable for both formal and informal occasions. The way a person wears their kimono is known as *kitsuke* (着付け, lit. 'dressing')

Previously Kimono was the most common Japanese garment, in the present day, it has fallen out of favor and is rarely worn as an everyday dress. Now they are frequently seen at summer festivals and people frequently wear the yukatas an informal type of kimono. Formal types of kimonos are worn to funerals, weddings, graduations, and other formal events. People who commonly wear kimonos include geisha, who are required to wear them as part of their profession.

Despite the low number of people who wear kimono regularly and the garment's reputation as a complicated article of clothing, the kimono has experienced several revivals in previous decades and is still worn today as fashionable clothing within Japan. Kimonos are very expensive starting around 10,000 yen 100 USD up to 1000000 yen 700 USD. In comparison Yukata costs between 30 and 100 USD.

Yukata (浴衣)

Yukata is a casual version of the kimono, made of cotton or synthetic fabric, wrapped around the body, and fastened with a sash. The name means "bathing cloth" which was its original use. Hotels and ryokans provide them for your use during your stay. We were provided with them when we stayed at the Tokyo Hilton Hotel.

Geisha

It seems that the concept of Geisha perpetuates several stereotypes in Western countries, especially about the sometimes-scorned role of these women. It is common for foreigners to give the wrong impression that they are escort girls or prostitutes. Which is far from the truth.

Originally, the Geisha term meant "practicing the arts". It was introduced in the middle of the 18th century when women were employed to entertain clients in tea houses known as お茶屋 "*ochaya*". They had to master several traditional arts such as music, dance, tea ceremony, floral arts, etc., and have good general knowledge for conversation with clients. The profession was officially recognized by the government in 1779 and prohibited prostitution and was forbidden in Japan and banned in 1957.

Through the years, their number decreased despite a small revival these past years. Today, they can be found almost exclusively in Kyoto, where they are known as 芸妓 *Geiko*, while their apprentices are called 舞妓 *Maiko*.

Geisha's costumes are made of a handmade silk kimono which can cost can over ¥500,000 / ~US$3,503) with a large belt of silk tied in their back, socks, and wooden sandals. Their faces are made up of white rice powder, up to the nape of their necks.

Gei-sha means the person of arts and *mai-ko* means the child who dances. The word *gei* refers to performing arts. *Mai* means "dance" and –ko in this context refers to a child.

Chapter 13

Japanese Arts and Crafts.

Many Japanese arts are common with other cultures both eastern and western such as Painting, Ceramics, Sculpture, Woodworking, Wood carving, etc. But there are some arts and crafts Japan is famous for, even though they migrated from other cultures like China and Korea such as: -

Ukiyo-e -- Wood block printing.
Kawara -- roofing tiles on Temples and Shrines.
Ikebana -- Flower arranging.
Bonsai -- Miniature trees.
Shikki -- Lacquerware.

Ukiyo-e

The most unique of these is known as "*Ukiyo*-e" which means "pictures of the floating world". This woodblock printing technique dates back to 1670 when *Hishikawa* made a monochrome print of a woman from one of his paintings. The color printing technique using several woodblock carvings came later in the 1760s, sometimes as many as 10 blocks are required to make an intricate print.

The technique flourished in the 17th-to–19th centuries, artists produced woodblock prints and paintings of subjects including women; kabuki actors, and sumo wrestlers. Scenes from history and folk tales; travel scenes and landscapes; Japanese flora and fauna; and erotica.

Ukiyo-e of "Great Wave of Kanagawa"

The most famous and copied print was by the well-known artist *Katsushika Hokusai* around 1830 called "The Great Wave of Kanagawa". The print depicts three boats moving through a storm-tossed sea with a large wave forming a spiral in the center and Mount Fuji visible in the background. His other well-known work is a series called "Thirty-six Views of Mount Fuji". His work inspired several notable artists such as including Van Gogh, Debussy, and Monet.

Hokusai was born as the son of a "shogun "and began painting when he was six years old, and when he was sixteen, he became an engraver's apprentice which was the beginning of his creative work. A couple of years later was an apprentice to great ukiyo-e artist *Katsukawa Shunshō* and after that Hokusai created several woodblock prints.

Of course, many other artists created ukiyo-e who makes woodblock prints of Japanese scenes even today. Often Wood blocks are carved by wood carvers from images created by the artist and printed on hand-made paper.

Roofing tiles

Other unique crafts in Japan that migrated from China and Korea are roofing tiles. These intricate tiles and other ornaments can be seen on temples and shrines created by specialist craftsmen.

They are known as "Kawara" oven-baked clay roof tiles dating back to the late 6th century. There are several shapes of *kawara* tiles used on roofs. They arrived in Japan around the same time as Buddhism and the end tiles were decorated with floral designs such as lotus blooms relating to Buddhism, later they took on various other shapes.

The most commonly decorated tiles are those that cap the ends of the eaves, corners, or ridgeline of a roof. They seal the structure to prevent water leakage, wear and tear. Eaves are capped with round disks, known as *gatou*, joined by broad, semi-circular tile endings called *nokihiragawara. Onigawara* is found at the ends of the main roof ridge. Sometimes they have grotesque images. *Ohmune*, and at the ends of the descending ridges. *Kudarimune* and its practical purpose are to protect against weathering, and though primarily made of ceramic.

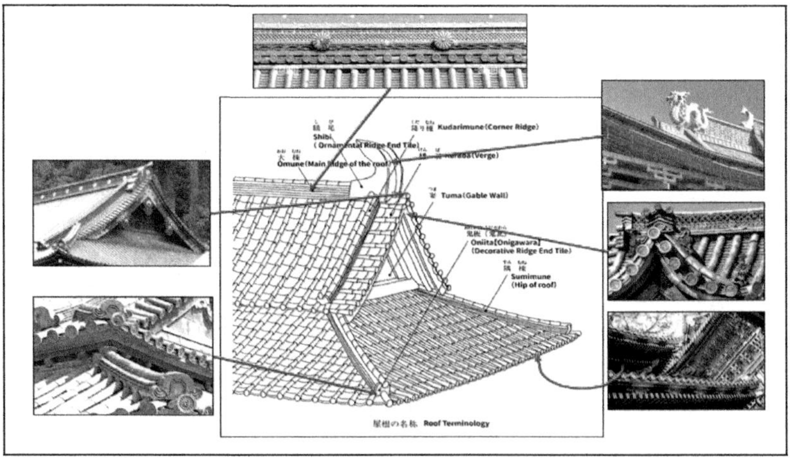

Roofing Technology

Other Japanese Arts

As in all other cultures japan practices many art forms. Some common with the west and others unique to Japan or migrated from China, Taiwan, and Korea such as: -.

Painting
Ikebana and Bonsai
Textile
Pottery
Lacquerware
Painting (*Kaiga* 絵画 and *Gado* 画道)

Sliding doors

Movable screen

In all cultures around the world, paintings were created as a means of communication and record keeping and date back to the prehistoric period. Japan is no exception, Painting can be seen in temples in Nara created during the Nara Period (710-794).

The oldest of the Japanese visual arts, painting, is complex and highly varied. Its history has been influenced by Chinese and western art, and some of its most popular subjects are religion, landscapes, ideograms, birds, and flowers. Chinese influence was mainly of religious images with the arrival of Buddhism.

During the Meiji period, Japanese traditional painting was called nihonga, mostly to distinguish it from western painting. The main difference lies in the materials used. The painting is done on a base made of paper, silk, wood, or plaster; and the colors come from natural pigments.

The other visual difference between Japanese and Western paintings is the style. Most Japanese paintings tend to be line drawings depicting natural objects or scenery compared to western paintings are more pictorial like a photograph. To master the painting technique, a long training is often necessary. These paintings can be seen in houses and other public places. An example shown above is a painting of a plum tree on a set of sliding doors from the 17th century.

This kind of drawing can also be found on moveable and fixed folding screens. The ink-on-paper work depicts a view of Japanese pine trees in the mist, with parts of the trees visible and parts obscured, illustrating the Zen Buddhist concept of ma (間) meaning gaps or open spaces in drawings or ikebana flower arrangements. Evoking the aesthetic of rustic simplicity, considered to be the first painting to depict only trees as subject matter.

Another example of a painting in black ink is seen here by the artist Sesshu Toyo from around 1470 influenced by Buddhism. A temple and snow-covered mountains can be seen in layers

Ikebana 生け花, 活け花,

Ikebana means "arranging flowers" or "making flowers alive" It is the art of flower arrangement. It is also known as kadō "way of flowers". The tradition dates back to the Heian period when floral offerings were made at altars. Later, flower arrangements were instead used to adorn the alcove of a traditional Japanese home.

Barb's Ikebana creation

Ikebana reached its peak in the 16th century under the influence of Buddhist tea masters and has grown over the centuries to a multitude of distinct styles.

Ikebana is counted as one of the three classical Japanese arts of refinement, along with *kōdō* for incense appreciation and *chadō* for tea and the tea ceremony. Barb attended Ikebana classes while we were in Japan. Here is one of her creations. She also brought back a vase made especially for Ikebana.

Bonsai

Bonsai is the Japanese art of growing and training miniature trees in pots, developed from the traditional Chinese art form of *penjing*. Unlike *penjing*, the Japanese "bonsai" only attempts to produce small trees that mimic the shape of real-life trees. Similar versions of the art exist in other cultures, such as Vietnamese. The art dates back to the 6th century practiced by Buddhist students.

Textiles

Japan is not unique in its history of Textile and fabric development. However, there are some aspects of weaving and dying techniques integral to the development of a unique fashion culture epitomized by the kimono.

The earliest known raw material for making fabric was considered to be hemp. Later during the Yayoi period, in 300 CE silk came to use drawing on the techniques introduced by China and Korea.

As fabric weaving skills developed, the materials and techniques used for making clothes came to reflect the wearer's social class. In the seventh and eighth centuries, for example, ornate *mon-orimono* (meaning fabric woven with patterns) silken garments were worn by the aristocracy. Robes with long hemlines and wide sleeves represented authority, influenced by the customs of China.

Junihitoe, the formal court dress of women at this time comprising multiple layers of colorful mon-orimono, is representative of this style. On the other hand, common folk mainly wore clothing made from hemp, until cotton became common in the seventeenth century.

The *jūnihitoe* (十二単) meaning 'twelve layers' is a style of formal court dress first worn around the 10th century by noble women and "ladies-in-waiting" at the Japanese Imperial Court. Even though the name implies twelve layers the number of layers varied. It consisted of layers of robes on top of each other. The outer layers are cut away and thinner to reveal the layered garments underneath. It is these outer layers with short wide sleeves that eventually developed into the modern-day kimono.

Today the jūnihitoe is still worn by members of the Imperial House of Japan on important occasions. Several companies in Japan specialize in these exotic textiles and garments.

Pottery, Ceramics, and Porcelain

Again, pottery evolved in all cultures of the world. However, there are a few examples of ceramics that are unique to Japan. According to UNESCO World Heritage, the oldest ceramics in the world were found in an archeological site in northern Japan dating back to the *Jo(h)mon* period 15,000 years ago.

As with most early art forms, each region developed its style of making Japanese ceramics with unique aesthetics based on the type of clay in the area, the glaze used, and the firing methods. Here are a few examples of popular styles. Some of the techniques originated in Korea and China.

Imari-Arita ware

Imari-Arita ware

It is considered that the kilns set up in the 17th century in Arita in the izen province of Kyushu island formed the heart of the Japanese porcelain industry after kaolin was discovered in 1616. Some kilns began to produce revised Korean-style blue and white porcelains, known as Early Imari. In the mid-17th a Chinese refugee in northern Kyushu brought the overglaze enamel coloring technique to Arita. In the 1640s, ceramics with a red design named aka-e became the symbol of the Kakiemon-style ceramic. By 1688, another important style appeared: *kinrande*, featuring gold and red patterns. In 1870, *gosu* porcelain developed, using cobalt as a raw material.

Imari-Arita ware is delicate and lightweight, with excellent durability. Its fine transparent white porcelain, and its colors, indigo, bright red, and sometimes gold, make it easily recognizable.

Tokoname ware (常滑)

Tokoname ware

Pottery made in *Tokoname* dates back to the 12th century. During the Heian period. Tokoname ware was already part of daily life. A kiln known as the *Takasaka* was built in the 14th century. Towards the end of the Edo period in the late 19th century, A potter called *Koie Hokyu* completed a multi-chambered kiln called a "climbing kiln". The excellent reputation of modern Tokoname ware was established by his son. He laid the foundations for earthenware pipe making and introduced the redware for which the town became renowned. A statue was later put up in his honor in the town. The traditions behind Tokoname ware have been kept alive by generations of potters. In 1998, third-generation potter was named a Living National Treasure.

Mikawachi ware

Mikawachi

Mikawachi ware was developed around the city of Sasebo in Nagasaki during the end of the 16th century when the lord of the *Hirado* domain brought several Korean potters to Japan, including an artisan named *Koseki.* Around the year 1640, the white porcelain mineral was discovered by Koseki's son.

Around the year 1650, businesses set up kilns to manufacture Mikawachi ware throughout the Hirado domain. They were often presented as gifts to the Edo shogunate and exported to territories like China and Europe. These Japanese potteries were sometimes known as Hirado ware

Mikawachi ware was considered as high-quality item due to the blue dye on white porcelain. Patterns such as Children playing are often depicted on these. During the Ming dynasty pictures of young boys meant prosperity and happiness.

There are as many as 32 types of Pottery ware produced throughout Japan a few are listed below: -

Seto ware, Aichi Prefecture

Seto ware dates back even further than its Arita discussed above and is considered one of the six ancient kilns in Japan. While other regions were still producing unglazed items, Seto ceramists had adopted glazing in creating more sturdy earthenware. Later during the Meiji period, they learned the technique of blue and white pottery from Arita.

Seto ware

Mino ware, Gifu Prefecture

Mino ware comes from several Gifu cities close to Seto, the most productive area in Japan for ceramics. The rich reserves of clay and the migration of the talented Seto ware makers to Mino to evade the wars.

Shigaraki ware, Shiga Prefecture

Shigaraki ware is an ancient kiln in Japan known for its quality in firing different types of clay to produce natural beauty with a coarser surface with burn marks and white dots. The tiles made by the kilns were used by the emperor in his residence.

Bizen ware, Okayama Prefecture

Similar to Shigaraki ware above unpolished texture can be seen on unglazed Bizen ware. The clay is dug up from deep underground and has to be stored for a couple of years before use. Fired at a temperature of 1,300°C to create unique patterns

Karatsu ware, Saga Prefecture

Karatsu ware was brought by migrating Korean craftsmen to Japan in the 16th century and inherited the elegant appearance of the mid-Joseon Dynasty in Korea.

Kutani ware, Ishikawa Prefecture

Kutani ware has a defining character in the variety of colors from the clay and stones rich in Iron. Enabling compositions of images and patterns are in red, green, yellow, purple, and blue.

Onta ware, Ōita Prefecture

Onta ware does not have a long history like the others, just about 300 years. The claystone is ground using river water to power the mill. It gained nationwide popularity in the 1930s after a campaign by Folk Art movement founder *Yanagi Sōetsu.*

Lacquerware (漆器, shikki)

It has been confirmed that the lacquer tree existed in the Jōmon period by radioactive carbon dating of the lacquer tree found at the *Torihama* shell mound, and is the oldest lacquer tree in the world. Lacquer was used in Japan as early as 7000 BCE, during the Jōmon period.

These trees found in China, Japan, and Korea are cultivated and the toxic sap is tapped to coat articles made of wood, clay, metal, etc.

Writing box with Maki-e

Lacquerware is a Japanese craft with a wide range of fine and decorative arts, lacquer has been used in prints on wood blocks, and other objects from religious statues and food boxes that are known as obento

The characteristic of Japanese lacquerware is the diversity of lacquerware using a decoration technique called *maki*-e in which metal powder is sprinkled to attach to lacquer. The invention of various maki-e techniques expanded artistic expression, tools, and works of highly decorative art such as *inro.*

17th century Tiered

Several terms are used to refer to lacquerware. Such as Shikki means "lacquerware", while *nurimono* means "coated things", and *urushi-nuri* means "lacquer coating."

European imitation of lacquer finish is known as Japanning first used on furniture and later on small items in metal, clay, etc. Sometimes they are called "Toleware" from the French tôle peinte, meaning "painted sheet metal".

Japanese artifacts in our home

We brought several items of Japanese art and craft back after our short stay as seen in the images below.

Japanese sideboard filled with Japanese items

Japanese Dining Table

Wall Screen by Shun-sen 1886

Woodblock print

Chapter 13

Japanese food.

Since most people are familiar with Japanese food, below are brief descriptions of the most common modern food found in restaurants. Included here is what we have eaten while we were in Japan in restaurants.

Sushi

It is one of the first foods that spring to mind when we think about Japanese food. The word 'sushi' refers to any dish made with Japanese rice that has been seasoned with rice vinegar. Common varieties of sushi include *makizushi* rice with fillings rolled up in seaweed, nigiri a bite-size ball of rice with single slices of raw fish or similar draped over the top and inarizushi is rice stuffed inside pockets of seasoned fried tofu.

Sushi

Sashimi

It is raw fish or meat that has been cut into thin slices and served with daikon radish, pickled ginger, wasabi, and soy sauce. The difference between sashimi and sushi is that sushi is made with rice and may not contain raw fish or meat. Fish and meat used for sashimi must be fresh and uncontaminated.

Sashimi

Udon

It is one of the three main noodle varieties of noodle which are thick, chewy, and traditionally made from wheat flour and brine water. It is usually served in mixed with stir-fries, often served in a savory soup broth fried tofu, or tempura.

Udon

Tempura

They are pieces or slices of meat, fish, and/or vegetables that have been covered in a special tempura batter and deep-fried until they become crunchy and pale gold in color. They are different from battered fish fry but are made from small shellfish like prawns, or vegetables like green beans, pumpkin, daikon radish, and sweet potato. Tempura can be eaten by itself or on top of bowls of rice or noodle soups.

Tempura

Yakitori

Similar to takeaway foods like fish fry in the UK, a similar favorite food in Japan is yakitori, which means barbecued chicken. They are small skewers of bite-size chicken pieces seasoned with salt or brushed with a sauce, or tare, of mirin rice wine, soy sauce, sake alcohol, and sugar. There are many different types of yakitori, but the most common is chicken.

Yakitori

Ramen

Ramen is a soup made with a savory broth of soy sauce, salt miso, and pork bone with wheat noodles in a deep bowl. Usually with toppings of meat, protein, and/or vegetables such as sliced pork, seaweed, spring onions, bamboo shoots, and others. It is one of Japan's absolute favorite delicacies, costing very little and being widely available in restaurants and ramen bars on almost every street corner.

Ramen

Donburi

This rice bowl dish is a common lunchtime choice among busy Japanese workers. It is made by preparing by simmering or frying meat, fish and vegetables served over steamed rice in a large bowl. The most common types include simmered chicken, egg, and green onion, sliced beef, and onion simmered in a soy sauce soup base, sometimes fried tempura pieces and breaded and deep-fried pork cutlets, or tonkatsu, simmered in with onion and egg are added.

Donburi

Soba

Soba is one of the three main types of noodles frequently eaten in Japan. It means "buckwheat" which is a type of wheat that grows in Japan and China. Noodles are made with buckwheat seed flour giving them a nutty flavor. Usually, it is served with soup with toppings of spring onions, seaweed, etc.

Soba

Tonkatsu

Tonkatsu is one of the foods that was introduced by Europeans. It is a pork cutlet that is coated with crispy breadcrumbs and frying them until they are golden brown. They are normally served with a sauce and shredded cabbage and other crisp salad greens on the side. Tonkatsu is often enjoyed as part of a bento-boxed lunch.

Tonkatsu

Sukiyaki

It is a hot pot dish commonly enjoyed during the winter prepared by searing beef slices in the hot pot, then adding sukiyaki broth made from soy sauce, sake, mirin rice wine and sugar vegetables, noodles, and proteins. The name 'sukiyaki' means 'cook what you like'. Sukiyaki is prepared on the dining table with friends and family.

Sukiyaki

Miso Soup

Made from a combination of miso paste made from fermented soybeans and dashi broth. It is the most common soup that is served as a side dish with traditional breakfasts, lunches, and dinners. To give the miso soup a little more body, several complementary toppings such as green onion, wakame seaweed, and firm tofu are added.

Miso soup

Shabu-shabu

The name "Shabu-shabu" comes from the noise it makes when the hot pot boils. It is a hot pot dish similar to sukiyaki, made by boiling vegetables, tofu, and other ingredients in a mellow broth seasoned with sea kelp usually in a restaurant next to the table. Thin slices of meat are dipped into the broth and swished around for about 15 seconds until it cooks. The meat is then dipped in (ponzu) a citrus-seasoned soy sauce or sesame sauce before being eaten with some of the other boiled ingredients.

Shabu-shabu

Onigiri

Onigiri is the Japanese equivalent of a sandwich a portable food many countries eat when traveling or a quick lunch. It is a rice ball with a filling in the center with pickled plums, seaweed mayonnaise, and Teriyaki chicken.

Onigiri

They cost between 100 and 150 yen around one USD.

Yakisoba

Yakisoba stands are popularly found everywhere during the summer and festivals. It is a fried noodle dish made by barbecuing or stir-frying a combination of noodles, sliced cabbage, port, carrots, and other vegetables. The ingredients are thrown onto a hot plate and barbecued. The name means "cooked" (yaki) "soba". Soba used is not noodles made from buckwheat.

Teppanyaki

The word is derived from the words *teppan* - metal plate, *Yaki* -- cook, to cook on a metal plate. They are very popular in western cities. The food is cooked in front of the customers on the table by an experienced chef who performs various tricks with the food and the utensils. The metal plate set into the table is heated by gas burners underneath the plate. Teppanyaki can be confused with yakisoba or hibachi. Common foods cooked are rice, noodles, eggs, and chopped vegetables.

Teppanyaki

Edamame

snacks like peanuts, crisps, etc. consumed at bars as an appetizer with a drink or before a meal. Edamame is the Japanese equivalent of a snack served as a complimentary appetizer before the meal. They are young

Edamame

immature soybean pods blanched and lightly salted seasoning.

Restaurants

Restaurants that offer traditional Japanese foods are served from simple bar-like counters with a line of chairs for the diners. The chefs stand behind the counter and cook and serve the food fresh based on customers' orders. Some of them do have tables and chairs. Here is the famous Chef Jiro and his son in their Tokyo Sushi restaurant with President Obama and Japanese politicians.

Jiro sushi restaurant

Izakaya

people go to drink and eat from late afternoon. It combines features of French bistros, restaurants and Spanish tapas bars. People love to gather with friends or colleagues in these shops squeezed in *yokocho* meaning alleyways or side streets, near the train stations. They are a little like pubs in the UK. But *izakaya* the *izakaya* are distinctive happy hours establishments with deep local roots. The concept appeared during the Edo period (1603 – 1868) when *nihonshu* (Sake) makers offered their customers to taste their drinks directly on the production site, seated at a table. The 3 *kanji* characters used for the word *izakaya* 居酒屋 can therefore be translated as "dinner at an alcohol shop," a place where one can eat and drink

Open only in the evening, the *izakaya* welcome employees for a relaxing after work and socializing. Salary-men used to be the main customers of these establishments, now a varied adult population 20 years and older are clients of these bars, including women, students or retirees.

nomikai (飲み会) is an informal meeting of colleagues to drink together.
bonenkai (忘年会) parties to celebrate the end of the year in December, and
shinnenkai (新年会) for a good start of the year

After settling down at the tables the custom is to start a round of Japanese beer clink the glasses and yell *Kanpai!* to toast together. There is a large choice of drinks Most popular drinks are:

There is usually no coffee and very few imported drinks like French wines or English beers.

Typical dishes of Japanese cuisine, such as:

- *Edamame* soy bean;
- *Yakitori* skewered grilled meat;
- Fritters: chicken *karaage*, *korokke*, fried tofu, *tempura*;
- Raw fish in *sashimi* or *maki-zushi*;
- Grilled fish;
- *Gyoza* dumplings;
- *Tamagoyaki* omelet; and,

Japanese *nabe* hotpot for which the ingredients are cooked at the table.

Usually a table fee, called *otoshidai* (お通し代) is be charged upon seating on average ¥500. To compensate, a side dish called otoshi is served, as an appetizer. Typically tipping is not necessary in Japan.

The most cost effective is the all you can eat and drink options. Known as "*Tabehodai*" and "*Nomihoda*. Usually there is a time limit for the "all-you-can": around 2 hours, with the last order to be made 90 minutes before closing time, and the drinks and dishes must be among a selection made by the place.

Chapter 14

Other unique aspects of Japan.

Accommodation

There are several types of hotels that are unique to Japan other than modern western hotels like Hilton, Business Hotels, or apartments for rent.

They are: -*Ryokan, Minshuku*, Capsule Hotels, Love Hotels, Temple lodgings, etc.

Ryokan/Minshuku

They are traditional Japanese-style inns with traditional Japanese-style rooms. Accommodation typically includes dinner and breakfast. Sometimes they include hot spring baths known as "*Onsen*". We stayed in a Ryokan when we visited the Izu Peninsula. They are very comfortable and value for money. Minshukus are similar to Ryokans usually cheaper family-run Japanese-style bed and breakfast lodgings, often include one or two meals.

Rvokan

Capsule Hotel

They were originally targeted toward male business clients known as "salarymen" who may have missed the last train or drunk after a business dinner. They are small boxes like long rooms about a meter wide and two meters long with a bed and a television. They cannot be reserved in advance. Typically costing around 3500 yen.

Capsule Hotel

Love hotels

Love hotels or fashion hotels that offer double rooms for short periods, for a minimum of one to three hours during the day, called a "rest", or for the whole night, called a "stay", which usually starts after 10 pm. The main purpose is to provide couples with a room to spend some undisturbed time together. The typical cost is 6000 to 12000 yen.

Temple Lodgings

Some Buddhist temples offer overnight accommodation known as *shukubo.* Often, they include two vegetarian meals and the guests can join the morning prayers

Festivals (Matsuri)

Matsuris are traditional festive occasions often celebrated with dance and music in Japan.

Most famous is the Children's festival known as *Shichi-go-san* meaning Seven - Five -Three observed on November 15th celebrated by girls three and seven and boys five years old. They are taken to Shinto shrines and offer thanks.

Bon-Odori in July 13th to 15th annual festival is for honoring the spirits of family ancestors who have passed away.

There are several others such as the Sapporo Snow Festival, Takayama Matsuri with elaborately decorated floats,

Aoi Matsuri celebrates the Henan Period and several celebrate Shinto Shrines and Buddhist temples usually held in Kyoto.

ABOUT THE AUTOR

Kiri is an amateur author who enjoys writing in his spare time on subjects that are interests to him, his family and friends. Born in Sri Lanka and has lived and worked in Sri Lanka, United Kingdom, Japan and United States. His books are factual and based on his personal experience and of his friends and family. He has published a book based on his overland car trip from England to Sri Lanka with two of his friends in 1970. His is a retired Engineers and enjoys volunteer work and writing in his retirement.

INDEX

Aso -- A mountain in Kyushu

Auska-- Prehistoric period around 538 -710 CE

Bonsai Art of growing miniature trees

Daibutsu Great statue of Buddha

Daimyōs Rulers

Dibutsuden Great Buddha hall built in 1709 AD

Fusuma Sliding doors made with wooden frames covered with translucent paper called washi

Futon Portable sleeping mattress and a cover for sleeping on the floor

Geisha Meaning practicing the arts. They were women employed to entertain customers in tea houses

Genkan Entrance hall in a house

Geta Japanese wooden slippers

Hara-kiri Practice of suicide by cutting in to the stomach

Hieizan Warrior monks around 1571 AD

Hiragana Japanese alphabet used to enhance kanji characters by adding them after the Kanji character

Ikebana Art of flower arrangement

Ikkō-Ikkii-- A group of rebels backed by Buddhist temple in 1580

Jo(h)mon A period in early Japan 15,000 years ago

Kanji Chinese characters derived from pictograms

Katakana Second Japanese alphabet used to write imported languages such as English

Kawara Roofing tiles on temples and shrines

Kimono Meaning item to wear, traditional national Japanese dress

Kokyo Imperial palace in Tokyo

Komainu Statues of animals placed by the tori gates to ward off evil spirits

Kondo Single story hipped tiled roof known as Classic Golden Hall in Nara

Kōsoku-dōro Metropolitan expressway in Tokyo

Kotatsu A blanket used with a dining table to keep legs and feet warm

Maiko Apprentice geisha

Minshuku Lodging with meals run by a family, also known as a pension

Mitsuhide A group leader who defeated Nobunaga a ruthless ruler 9n 1580

Mochi Rice cake

Nihon-go Japanese language a member of Japonic languages

Ochoko Nickname for sake cup

Ofuro Communal bath tub

Onsen Hot spring baths

Romon Entrance to a Buddhist temple

Ryokan, A traditional Japanese hotel with rooms and food

Sakazuki Small cup for drinking sake

Samurai Japanese solders belonging to a shogun

Seisen	Name if a girl's school in Setagaya, Tokyo
Sekigahara	Name of a battle and location in 1600
Shichi-go-san	A festival held for children of seven, five and three
Shikki	Lacquerware
Shinkansen	New main line -- popularly known as the bullet train
Shogun	Military and Political leader
Shuto	Name of capital city expressway
Tamagawa Dori	Name of a road in Tokyo- Dori means road
Tatami	A thick floor mat made with woven straw
Temozuya	A tank of water in temples for cleansing before entering
Tenmangu	Shinto shrine 845 - 903 AD in Nara
Tera Or Ji	Meaning a Buddhist temple
Tokoname	Pottery made in the 12th century
Tokugawa Ieyasu	A Shogun who was known as the great unifier in 1600s
Tori	Entrance gate to generally a shrine
Tosho Daigongen	Great Deity of the East Shining Light as Ieyasu' s mausoleum
Toshogu	Memorial Shrine build for Shogun Tokugawa Ieyasu in Nikko
Ukiyo-e	Meaning picture of the floating world -- wood block printing
Washitsu	A multi-purpose tatami mat room in a house
Yaoi --	Prehistoric period around 300 CE
Yukata	A dressing gown worn for relaxing and after a bath

Printed in Great Britain
by Amazon

23260250R00066